Rick Steves'

SNAPSHOT

Naples & the Amalfi Coast

CONTENTS

INTRODUCTION

This Snapshot guide, excerpted from the latest edition of my guidebook *Rick Steves' Italy*, introduces you to Naples and the Amalfi Coast. The gritty, historic port city of Naples is arguably Italy's wildest urban jungle, with a uniquely vibrant street life. Enjoy a pizza in its birthplace, and explore the city's excellent Archaeological Museum. Then head into the countryside to unearth ancient history at Pompeii and Herculaneum, well-preserved Roman towns in the shadow of the steaming Mt. Vesuvius.

An hour to the south, Sorrento kicks off the gloriously scenic Amalfi Coast, where buses filled with white-knuckle tourists take turns squeezing along an impossibly narrow sea-view road. Relax in stylish Sorrento, hilly Positano, or low-key Amalfi, and side-trip to the ancient Greek temples at Paestum, or to the jet-set isle of Capri, with its otherworldly Blue Grotto.

To help you have the best trip possible, I've included the following topics in this book:

• **Planning Your Time,** with advice on how to make the most of your limited time

• **Orientation,** including tourist information (abbreviated as TI), tips on public transportation, local tour options, and helpful hints

• **Sights** with ratings:

▲▲▲—Don't miss

▲▲—Try hard to see

▲—Worthwhile if you can make it

No rating—Worth knowing about

• **Sleeping** and **Eating,** with good-value recommendations in every price range

• **Connections,** with tips on trains, buses, and driving

• **Practicalities,** near the end of this book, has information on money, phoning, hotel reservations, transportation, and other helpful hints, plus Italian survival phrases.

To travel smartly, read this little book in its entirety before you go. It's my hope that this guide will make your trip more meaningful and rewarding. Traveling like a temporary local, you'll get the absolute most out of every mile, minute, and euro.

Buon viaggio!

Rick Steves

NAPLES

Napoli

If you like Italy as far south as Rome, go farther south—it gets better. If Italy is getting on your nerves, don't go farther. Italy intensifies as you plunge deeper. Naples is Italy in the extreme—its best (birthplace of pizza and Sophia Loren) and its worst (home of the Camorra, Naples' "family" of organized crime). Just beyond Naples you'll find the impressive ruins of Pompeii and Herculaneum...and the brooding volcano that did them both in, Mount Vesuvius.

Neapolis ("new city") was a thriving Greek commercial center 2,500 years ago. Today, it remains southern Italy's leading city, offering a fascinating collection of museums, churches, and eclectic architecture. Walking through its colorful Old Town is one of my favorite sightseeing experiences anywhere in Italy.

Naples—Italy's third-largest city, with more than one million people—has almost no open spaces or parks, which makes

its position as Europe's most densely populated city plenty evident. Watching the police try to enforce traffic sanity is almost comical in Italy's grittiest, most polluted, and most crime-ridden city. But Naples surprises the observant traveler with its impressive knack for living, eating, and raising children in the streets with good humor and decency. Overcome your fear of being run down or ripped off long enough to talk with people. Enjoy a few smiles and jokes with the man running the neighborhood tripe shop, or the woman taking her day-care class on a walk through the traffic.

The pulse of Italy throbs in Naples. Like Cairo or Mumbai, it's appalling and captivating at the same time, the closest thing to "reality travel" that you'll find in Western Europe. But this tangled mess still somehow manages to breathe, laugh, and sing—with a captivating Italian accent.

Planning Your Time

Naples makes an ideal day trip either from Rome or from the comfortable home base of Sorrento, located an hour south (see next chapter)—although I've listed a few accommodations for those who want to stay overnight here.

On a quick visit, start with the Archaeological Museum (closed Tue), follow my "A Slice of Neapolitan Life" self-guided walk, and celebrate your survival with pizza. Of course, Naples is huge. But even with limited time, if you stick to the prescribed route and grab a cab when you're lost or tired, it's fun. Treat yourself well in Naples; the city is cheap by Italian standards.

For a blitz tour from Rome, you could have breakfast on an early Rome-Naples express train (for example, Mon-Fri 7:35-8:45), do Naples and Pompeii in a day, and be back in Rome in time for bed. That's exhausting, but more memorable than a fourth day in Rome.

Remember that in the afternoon, Naples' street life slows and many sights close as the temperature soars. The city comes back to life in the early evening.

Orientation to Naples

Naples is set deep inside the large and curving Bay of Naples, with Mount Vesuvius looming just five miles away. Although Naples is a sprawling city, its fairly compact core contains the most interesting sights. The tourist's Naples is a triangular shape, from the Centrale train station to the east, the Archaeological Museum to the west, and the Piazza del Plebiscito (Royal Palace) and port to the south. Within this triangle are unusual churches and a very straight street.

Tourist Information

The most convenient of Naples' three TIs is in the **Centrale** train station (daily 9:00-19:00, near track 23, tel. 081-268-779, www .inaples.it). Pick up a map and the *Qui Napoli* booklet, which lists the latest museum hours, events, and transportation info; if the staff says the booklets are "finished," ask for an old one. In town, you'll find TIs at the **Galleria Umberto I shopping mall** (across

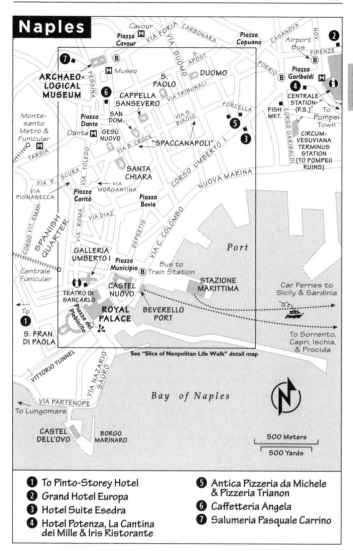

Naples

Cavour
Piazza M Cavour
Piazza Capuana
Airport Bus
FIRENZE
B
VIA FORIA
CARBONARA
CASANOVA
NOV
2
B
Piazza
POERIO
B Garibaldi M
Museo M
S. APOST
DUOMO
ARCHAEO-LOGICAL MUSEUM
7
PELLE
VIA DUOMO
S. PAOLO
CAPPELLA SANSEVERO
6
CENTRALE STATION (F.S.)
4
i
Monte-santo Metro & Funicular
Piazza Dante
SAN DOM.
VIA TRIBUNALI
VIA S. BIAGIO
FORCELLA
FISH MKT.
To Pompei Town
M
Dante M
GESÙ NUOVO
VIA B. CROCE
"SPACCANAPOLI"
5
3
CIRCUM-VESUVIANA TERMINUS STATION (TO POMPEII RUINS)
TARSIA
VIA P.
SCURA TOLEDO
SANTA CHIARA
CORSO UMBERTO I
NUOVA MARINA
VIA PIGNASECCA
VIA MORGANTINA
Piazza Carità
Piazza Bovio
VIA ROMA
VIA DIAZ
DEPRETIS
VIA C. COLOMBO
Port
CORSO VIT. EMAN.
SPANISH QUARTER
GALLERIA UMBERTO I
Piazza Municipio
B
Bus to Train Station
Centrale Funicular
i
TEATRO DI SANCARLO
CASTEL NUOVO
STAZIONE MARITTIMA
Car Ferries to Sicily & Sardinia
To
1
Piazza del Plebiscito
ROYAL PALACE
BEVERELLO PORT
To Sorrento, Capri, Ischia, & Procida
S. FRAN. DI PAOLA
See "Slice of Neopolitan Life Walk" detail map
VITTORIO TUNNEL
VIA NAZARIO SAURO
Bay of Naples
N
VIA PARTENOPE
To Lungomare
CASTEL DELL'OVO
BORGO MARINARO
500 Meters
500 Yards

❶ To Pinto-Storey Hotel
❷ Grand Hotel Europa
❸ Hotel Suite Esedra
❹ Hotel Potenza, La Cantina dei Mille & Iris Ristorante
❺ Antica Pizzeria da Michele & Pizzeria Trianon
❻ Caffetteria Angela
❼ Salumeria Pasquale Carrino

from the entrance to the Teatro di San Carlo; Mon-Sat 9:00-19:00, Sun 9:00-14:00, tel. 081-402-394) and across from the **Church of Gesù Nuovo** (same hours as Galleria Umberto I, tel. 081-551-2701).

Arrival in Naples

By Train: There are several Naples train stations, but all trains coming into town stop at either Napoli Centrale or Garibaldi—essentially the same stop, one on top of the other.

Planning Your Time in the Region

On a quick trip, give the entire area—including Sorrento and Naples—a minimum of three days. With Sorrento as your sunny springboard (see next chapter), spend a day in Naples, a day exploring the Amalfi Coast, and a day split between Pompeii and the town of Sorrento. While Paestum (Greek temples), Mount Vesuvius, Herculaneum (an ancient Roman site like Pompeii), and the island of Capri are decent destinations, they are worthwhile only if you have more time. For a map, see page 83.

The **Campania ArteCard** regional pass may save you a few euros if you're here for a quick trip, using public transportation, and plan on going to Pompeii (€11), Herculaneum (€11), or the Naples Archaeological Museum (€6.50). There are several versions, which generally cover most sights and the public transportation in the area. The three-day Tutta la Regione version makes the most sense, including free entry to two sights (50 percent off others) and transportation within Naples, on the Circumvesuviana train, and on Amalfi Coast buses (€27, sold at Naples TIs and participating sights, activates on first use, expires three days later at midnight, www .campaniartecard.it).

Centrale is the busiest station, facing Naples' main square, Piazza Garibaldi. You'll find all the administrative facilities in Centrale, including a TI, an ATM (at Banco di Napoli near track 24), and a baggage check (€4/5 hours, then €0.60/hour, daily 7:00-23:00, marked *deposito bagagli*, near track 5 but may move). Note that services in this station tend to change location frequently.

Garibaldi is a subway station used by trains to make a quick stop as they barrel through. It's connected to the Centrale station by escalators. The Circumvesuviana stop, for commuter trains to Sorrento and Pompeii, is also on this level.

By Boat: Naples is a ferry hub with great boat connections to Sorrento, Capri, and other nearby destinations. Ferries use the smaller Port Beverello dock (called Molo Beverello), while cruise ships use the Stazione Marittima cruise-ship terminal. The two docks are side-by-side at the port on the southeast edge of downtown Naples, near Castel Nuovo and the grand square called Piazza del Plebiscito. In the covered area between the terminal buildings, you'll find cafés and various shops, including a tobacco shop (where you can buy bus tickets).

Whether arriving by ferry or cruise ship, you can get to the city center by taxi, bus, or on foot; the Alibus shuttle bus runs to the airport (the stop is a couple of blocks inland from the port, between Castel Nuovo and Teatro di San Carlo; see "By Plane," below). The **taxi** stand is in front of the port area; figure €12-15 to get to the train station. **Buses** #601 and the less-frequent #152 head to Piazza Garibaldi and the train station—where you can connect to trains to sights outside of town (6/hour, 15 minutes, buy €1.20 ticket at tobacco shop, validate ticket in yellow box on the bus as you board; with your back to the boats, head right toward the traffic lights—the bus stop is just beyond, on the busy street). Straight ahead across the road is a drab square called Piazza Municipio, with a bus stop to Naples' Archaeological Museum a half-block down on Via Agostino Depretis (#R4, departs every 10-15 minutes, ride six stops to Piazza Museo).

On foot, it's a seven-minute **walk**—past the gigantic Castel Nuovo—to Piazza del Plebiscito and the old city center: After crossing the busy street in front of the port, head up the ramp just to the right of the castle. At the top, angle left, past Teatro di San Carlo, to Piazza del Plebiscito. You could start my self-guided walk in reverse from here.

By Plane: Naples International Airport (Capodichino) is located four miles northeast of the city center (tel. 081-789-6111 for operator, tel. 848-888-777 for info, www.gesac.it). Alibus shuttle buses zip you from the airport to Naples' Centrale train station/Piazza Garibaldi in 15 minutes, and then head to the port for boats to Capri and Sorrento (daily 6:30-24:00, 3/hour, less frequent early and late, 30 minutes to the port, €3, pay driver, stops at train station and port only). Local bus #C58, which also goes into town, is cheaper but stops more frequently (2/hour, €1.20). It's tough to get a cabbie to use the meter from the airport, but a taxi ride should cost about €20.

To reach **Sorrento** from Naples Airport, take the direct Curreri bus (daily at 9:00, 11:00, 13:00, 14:30, 16:30, and 19:30; 1.5 hours, €10, pay driver, tel. 081-801-5420, www.curreriviaggi.it).

Helpful Hints

Theft Alert: Err on the side of caution. Don't venture into neighborhoods that make you uncomfortable. Walk with confidence, as if you know where you're going and what you're doing. Assume able-bodied beggars are thieves.

Stick to busy streets and beware of gangs of hoodlums. A third of the city is unemployed, and past local governments have set an example that the Mafia would be proud of. Assume con artists are more clever than you. Any jostle or commotion is probably a thief-team smokescreen. To keep bags safe, it's probably best to store them at the Centrale train station.

Always walk on the sidewalk (even if the locals don't)

and carry your bag on the side away from the street—thieves on scooters have been known to snatch bags as they swoop by. The less you have dangling from you (including cameras and necklaces), the better.

Perhaps your biggest risk of theft is while catching or riding the Circumvesuviana commuter train. If you're connecting from a major train, you'll be stepping from a relatively secure compartment into a crowded Naples subway filled with thieves hunting disoriented tourists with luggage. While I ride the Circumvesuviana comfortably and safely, each year I hear of many who get ripped off on this ride. You won't be mugged—just conned or pickpocketed. Especially late at night, the Circumvesuviana train is plagued by intimidating ruffians. For maximum safety and peace of mind, sit in the front car, where the driver will double as your protector.

Con artists may say you need to "transfer" by taxi to catch the Circumvesuviana; you don't. Anyone offering to help you with your bags is likely a thief, despite displayed credentials. There are no porters at the Centrale train station or in the lower level where the Circumvesuviana station is located. Wear your money belt, hang on to your bag, and don't display any valuables.

Traffic Safety: In Naples, red lights are discretionary, and pedestrians need to be wary, particularly of motor scooters. Smart tourists jaywalk in the shadow of bold and confident locals, who generally ignore crosswalks. Wait for a break in traffic, cross with confidence, and make eye contact with approaching drivers. The traffic will stop.

Travel Agency: Ontano Tours books train and boat tickets from a small office just inland from the new Galleria del Mare shopping center at Port Beverello (Mon-Sat 8:30-20:00, closed Sun, tel. 081-580-0340, www.ontanotour.it).

Local Guides: Pina Esposito specializes in art and archaeology, and does fine tours of Naples' excellent but somewhat hard-to-appreciate Archaeological Museum (€120/2 hours, 10 percent off with this book, confirm one week in advance, sometimes available on shorter notice, mobile 349-596-8251, annamaria esposito1@virgilio.it). The team at Mondo Guide offers private tours of the museum and city (tel. 081-751-3290, www.mondoguide.it, info@mondoguide.it). Both Pina and Mondo Guide are flexible and also lead tours of Capri, Pompeii, and the surrounding area.

Getting Around Naples

By Subway: Naples' subway, the Metropolitana, has two lines. Line 2, the main line, runs from the Centrale train station (catch

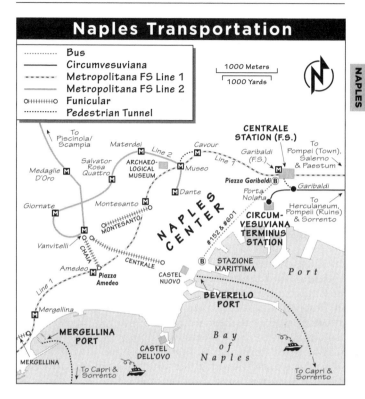

Naples Transportation

··········	Bus
——	Circumvesuviana
- - - - -	Metropolitana FS Line 1
——	Metropolitana FS Line 2
O++++++O	Funicular
··········	Pedestrian Tunnel

1000 Meters
1000 Yards

it downstairs at the Garibaldi stop) through the center of town (direction: Pozzuoli), stopping at Piazza Cavour (a five-minute walk from the Archaeological Museum) and Montesanto (top of Spanish Quarter and Spaccanapoli street). Line 1 runs from Piscinola/Scampia (suburbs) into the city center, stopping at the Museo station, near the Archaeological Museum (connects to Line 2's Piazza Cavour subway stop). Tickets cost €1.20 and are good for 1.5 hours. All-day tickets cost €3.60. Validate tickets either at the turnstile (if there is one), or in the small yellow boxes you'll see before you reach the track.

By Taxi: Taxi drivers in Naples are notorious for overcharging. A short ride in town should cost €10-12; figure on €12-15 from downtown to the port. Ask for the *tariffa predeterminata* (a fixed rate). There are some legitimate extra charges (baggage fees, €2 supplement after 22:00, €1.50 supplement on Sun and holidays).

By Bus: Buses are handy for getting between the port and train station. If you need to curtail my self-guided walk, you can hop a bus to the station. Tickets cost €1.20 at tobacco shops; validate the ticket in the yellow box on the bus as you board.

On a Hop-on, Hop-off Bus Tour: The "Sightseeing Napoli"

tour bus makes several different loops through the city, allow-ing riders to get on and off to explore, but Naples has only a few significant sights to see (€22, tickets good for 24 hours, buy from driver or from kiosk in front of Castel Nuovo near the port, scant recorded narration; for details, see the brochure at hotels and TI, www.napoli.city-sightseeing.it).

Self-Guided Tour

▲▲▲Archaeological Museum (Museo Archeologico)

For lovers of antiquity, this museum alone makes Naples a worth-while stop. Considering its popularity and the importance of the collection, it's remarkable how ramshackle, unkempt, and dumpy its displays are. Still, if you can overlook the dust bunnies, this museum offers the best possible peek into the artistic jewelry boxes of Pompeii and Herculaneum. When Pompeii was excavated in the early 1800s, Naples' Bourbon king bellowed, "Bring me the best

of what you find!" The actual sites are impressive but barren; the finest art and artifacts ended up here.

Cost and Hours: €6.50, but often €10 with mandatory charge for special exhibits, cash only, Wed-Mon 9:00-19:30, closed Tue.

Getting There: To take the subway from the Centrale train station, follow signs to the Metro, called *Metropolitana*, located downstairs at the Garibaldi subway station (across from track 13). Buy your ticket at the newsstand or a tobacco shop and ask which track—*"Quale binario?"* (KWAH-lay bee-NAH-ree-oh)—to Piazza Cavour (direction: Pozzuoli, usually track 4). Validate your ticket in the small yellow boxes near the escalator going down to the tracks. Hop on any train that comes through (confirm by its sign or with a local that it's going to the museum), and ride the subway one stop. As you leave the Metro, exit and hike five min-utes uphill along the busy street. Look for a grand old red building located up a flight of stairs at the top of the block.

If taking the Metro back to the Centrale station, exit the museum to the left, and continue downhill to the Cavour stop, passing the Museo station (which is on a different line).

Figure on €12 for a taxi from the train station to the museum.

Secret Room Appointment: Depending on how packed the museum is, you may need to make an appointment on arrival to

Rizzoli Bookstore
C'est Magnifique! E' Magnifico!
Es Magnifico! Rizzoli carries Italian

.

French, and Spanish Titles!
6/16/2012 4:53:03 PM
REG #: 7   CLERK #: 26   TRAN #: 16553
1@ $9.99 9781598806830   % $9.99T
RICK STEVES NAPLES AND THE AMALFI COAST

Sub-Total:	$9.99
Tax	$0.89
Total:	$10.88
Tendered: AMERICANEXPRESS	$10.88
XXXXXXXXXXXX3003 mmyy APPROVAL	559940
Reference No:	9290
Transaction Type:	Sale

31 W 57th Street New York NY 10019
(212)759-2424 rizzoliusa.com
No Cash Refunds, Exchange or Credit only

Rizzoli Bookstore
C'est Magnifique! È' Magnifico!
Es Magnifico! Rizzoli carries Italian

French, and Spanish Titles!
6/15/2012 4:53:03 PM
REG #: 7   CLERK #: 26   TRAN #: 16553
10   $9.99 9781598806830   % $9.99?
RICK STEVES NAPLES AND THE AMALFI COAST

Sub-Total:	$9.99
Tax	$0.89
Total:	$10.88
Tendered: AMERICANEXPRESS	$10.88
XXXXXXXXXXXXX3003 mmyy APPROVAL 555940	
Reference No:	9290
Transaction Type:	Sale

31 W 57th Street New York NY 10019
(212)759-2424 rizzoliusa.com
No Cash Refunds, Exchange or Credit only

visit the Secret Room (Gabinetto Segreto), which contains erotic art from Pompeii (included in admission, you get a 15-minute window; to schedule a time, go to the information counter—on your immediate left as you enter). When it's not crowded, an appointment is unnecessary.

Information: Tel. 081-442-2149. For the basics, you can follow my self-guided tour (below). If you want a **guided tour,** look for Pina Esposito at the museum (see "Helpful Hints," earlier; €120/2-hour tour, 10 percent less with this book; help her assemble a group of up to 10 to split the fee). **Audioguides,** which haven't been updated for years, cost €5 (at ticket desk). The shop sells a worthwhile *National Archaeological Museum of Naples* guidebook— at €12, it's still a better value than the audioguide. Bag check is obligatory and free. Photos are allowed without a flash.

The museum seems to be in constant chaos due to ongoing renovations. If you can't find a particular work, ask a museum custodian, *"Dov'è?"* (DOH-vay, meaning "Where is?"), followed by the item's name.

Overview

Entering the museum, stand at the base of the grand staircase. To your right, on the ground floor, are larger-than-life statues from the Farnese Collection, star-ring the *Toro Farnese*. Up the stairs on the mezzanine level (turn left at the lion) are mosaics and frescoes from Pompeii, including the *Battle of Alexander* and the Secret Room of erotic art. On the top floor is a scale model of Pompeii and bronze statues from Herculaneum (a nearby town destroyed in the same eruption that devastated Pompeii). You'll find WCs by circling behind the staircase.

• *From the base of the grand staircase, turn right and head to the far end.*

Ground Floor: The Farnese Collection

The museum's ground floor alone has enough Greek and Roman art to put any museum on the map. Its highlight is the Farnese Collection, a grand hall of huge, bright, and wonderfully restored statues excavated from Rome's Baths of Caracalla.

The tangled *Toro Farnese* depicts a woman being tied to a bull. At 13 feet, it's the tallest ancient marble group ever found, and the largest intact statue from antiquity. A third-century A.D. copy of a lost bronze Hellenistic original, it was carved out of one piece of marble. Michelangelo and others "restored" it at the pope's request—meaning that they integrated surviving bits into a new work. Panels on the wall show which pieces were actually carved by Michelangelo (in blue on the chart): the head of the woman in back, the torso of the aunt under the bull, and the dog. (Imagine how the statue would stand out if it was thoughtfully lit and not surrounded by white walls.)

Here's the story behind the statue: Once upon an ancient Greek time, King Lycus was bewitched by Dirce. He abandoned his pregnant wife, Antiope (standing regally in the background). The single mom gave birth to twin boys (shown here). When they grew up, they killed their deadbeat dad and tied Dirce to the horns of a bull to be bashed against a mountain. Captured in marble, the action is thrilling: cape flailing, dog

snarling, hooves in the air. You can almost hear the bull snorting. And in the back, Antiope oversees this harsh ancient justice with satisfaction.

At the far end of the hall stands **Hercules.** In a small room behind him is a glass case with the sumptuous **Farnese Cup** (*Tazza Farnese*, second century B.C., from Egypt). This large, ancient cameo made of agates looks less like a cup than a cereal bowl. Its decorations are both Egyptian (the Nile toting a lush cornucopia) and, on the flip side, Greek (Medusa's head).

• *Backtrack a bit, then head up to the mezzanine level.*

Mezzanine: Pompeiian Mosaics and the Secret Room

Most of these mosaics—of animals, musicians, and geometric designs—were taken from Pompeii's House of the Faun. The house's delightful centerpiece is a 20-inch-high statue of the *Dancing Faun* (which you'll find here, near the far room). This rare surviving Greek bronze statue (from the fourth century B.C.) is surrounded by some of the best mosaics of that age.

A museum highlight, just behind the statue, is the grand *Battle of Alexander,* a second-century B.C. copy of the original Greek fresco, done a century earlier. It decorated a floor in the House of the Faun and was found intact; the damage you see occurred as this treasure was moved from Pompeii to the king's

collection here. Alexander (left side of the scene, with curly hair and sideburns) is about to defeat the Persians under Darius (central figure, in chariot with turban and beard). This pivotal victory allowed Alexander to quickly overrun much of Asia (331 B.C.). Alexander is the only one without a helmet...a con-fident master of the battlefield while everyone else is fighting for

their lives, eyes bulging with fear. Notice how the horses, already in retreat, add to the scene's propaganda value. Notice also the shading and perspective, which Renaissance artists would later work so hard to accomplish. (A modern reproduction of the mosaic is now back in the House of the Faun.)

The **Secret Room** *(Gabinetto Segreto)* contains a sizable assortment of erotic frescoes, well-hung pottery, and perky stat-ues that once decorated bedrooms, meeting rooms, brothels, and even shops at Pompeii and Herculaneum. (On crowded days, you may have to make an appointment on arrival to view the room, though this is rare.) These bawdy statues and frescoes—many of them once displayed in Pompeii's grandest houses—were enter-tainment for guests. (By the time they made it to this museum, in 1819, the frescoes could be viewed only with permission from the king—see the letters in the glass case just outside the door.) The Roman nobles commissioned the wildest scenes imaginable. Think of them as ancient dirty jokes.

Circulating counterclockwise through this section, look for: 1) a faun playfully pulling the sheet off a beautiful woman, only to be grossed out by the plumbing of a hermaphrodite (perhaps the original *"Mamma mia!"*); 2) horny pygmies from Africa in action; 3) Venus, the patron goddess of Pompeii, a favorite pin-up girl; 4) a particularly high-quality statue of a goat and a satyr illustrating the act of sodomy; and 5) a toga with an embarrass-ing bulge.

The next room is furnished and decorated the way an ancient brothel might have been. The 10 frescoes on the wall functioned as both a menu of services offered and as a kind of *Kama Sutra* of sex positions. The walls feature big stone penises that once projected over Pompeii's doorways. A massive phallus was not necessarily a sexual symbol, but a magical amulet used against the "evil eye." It symbolized fertility, happiness, good luck, riches, straight A's, and general well-being. The glass cases contain more phallic art.

• *So, now that your travel buddy is finally showing a little interest in art...finish up your visit by climbing the stairs to the top floor.*

Top Floor: Statues, Artifacts, and a Model of Pompeii

At the top of the stairs, go through the center door to enter a grand, empty hall. This was the great hall of the university (17th and 18th centuries) until the building became the royal museum in 1777. The sundial (from 1791) still works. At noon, a sunray strikes the spot, indicating today's date...if you know your zodiac.

To your right are rooms containing **bronze statues** from Herculaneum—of racers, dancers, and fauns (first-century B.C. copies of fourth-century B.C. originals). They once decorated the holiday home (Villa dei Papyri in Herculaneum) of Julius Caesar's father-in-law. Look into the lifelike blue eyes of the intense *atleta* (athletes), bent on doing their best. The *Five Dancers,* with their inlaid-ivory eyes and graceful poses, decorated a portico. *Resting Hermes* (with his tired little heel wings) is taking a break. The *Drunken Faun* (singing and snapping

his fingers to the beat, a wineskin at his side) is clearly living for today—true to the *carpe diem* preaching of the Epicurean philosophy. Caesar's father-in-law was an Epicurean philosopher, and his library—containing 2,000 papyrus scrolls—supported his outlook.

Return to the grand hall and continue to the other side, passing through several rooms of vases, statuettes, spoons, glassware, and other objects found at Pompeii. Keep going to the far end, where you'll find a **scale model** of the archaeological site of Pompeii, circa 1879 *(plastico di Pompeii).* Belly up to the railing and find the Porta Marina entrance and the large rectangle of the town's Forum. Another model on the wall shows the site in 2004, after more excavations.

The Rest of the Museum

After years in restoration, the museum's large collection of **frescoes** taken from the walls of Pompeii villas is back (in Rooms LXVI to LXXVIII). Pompeiians loved to decorate their homes with scenes from mythology (Hercules' Labors, Venus and Mars in love), landscapes, everyday market scenes, and faux architecture.

The display is roughly chronological.

For extra credit, visit **Doriforo.** (Ask a guard, *"Dov'è il Doriforo?"* He was last spotted on the ground floor, in the hall to the left, as you face the staircase.) This seven-foot-tall "spear-carrier" (the literal translation of *doriforo*) just stands there, as if holding a spear. What's the big deal about this statue, which looks like so many others? It's a marble replica made by the Romans of one of the most-copied statues of antiquity, a fifth-century B.C. bronze Greek original by Polyclitus. This copy once stood in a Pompeii gym, where it inspired ancient athletes by showing the ideal proportions of Greek beauty. So full of motion, and so realistic in its *contrapposto* pose (weight on one foot), the *Doriforo* would later inspire Donatello

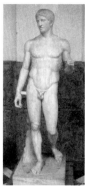

and Michelangelo, triggering the Renaissance. And so the glories of ancient Pompeii, once buried and forgotten, live on today.

Self-Guided Walk

▲▲▲A Slice of Neapolitan Life

Walk from the Archaeological Museum through the heart of town and back to the Centrale train station. Allow at least three hours, plus time for pizza and sightseeing stops. If you have limited time, do a shorter, hour-long version by walking briskly and skipping the sights south of Spaccanapoli (including the Royal Palace, Teatro di San Carlo, and Galleria Umberto I).

Naples, a living medieval city, is its own best sight. Couples artfully make love on Vespas surrounded by more fights and smiles per cobblestone than anywhere else in Italy. Rather than seeing Naples as a list of sights, visit its one great museum and then capture its essence by taking this walk through the core of the city. Should you become overwhelmed or lost, step into a store and ask for directions: "Where is Centrale station?" in Italian is *"Dov'è la stazione Centrale?"* (DOH-vay lah staht-zee-OH-nay chen-TRAH-lay). Or point to the next sight in this book.

Part 1: Via Pessina, Via Toledo, and the Spanish Quarter

The first part of this walk is a straight one-mile ramble down a boulevard to Galleria Umberto I, near the Royal Palace. Ideally, begin by touring the Archaeological Museum (at the top of Piazza Cavour, Metro: Cavour or Museo).

• *Leaving the Archaeological Museum, turn right and go one block, to the head of Via Pessina. Follow this busy street downhill to Piazza*

NAPLES

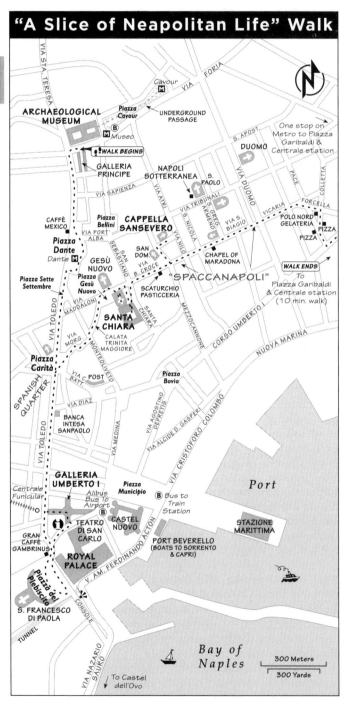

"A Slice of Neapolitan Life" Walk

- VIA STA. TERESA
- Cavour M
- VIA FORIA
- Piazza Cavour
- UNDERGROUND PASSAGE
- **ARCHAEOLOGICAL MUSEUM**
- B Museo
- S. APOST
- One stop on Metro to Piazza Garibaldi & Centrale station
- **DUOMO**
- VIA DUOMO
- PACE
- COLLETTA
- WALK BEGINS
- GALLERIA PRINCIPE
- NAPOLI SOTTERRANEA
- S. PAOLO
- VIA ATRI
- VIA TRIBUNALI
- VIA GREG ARMENO
- VIA S. BIAGIO
- VICARIA
- FORCELLA
- VIA SAPIENZA
- CAFFÈ MEXICO
- Piazza Bellini
- VIA PORT' ALBA
- **CAPPELLA SANSEVERO**
- VIA S. NICOLA
- VIA NILO
- POLO NORD GELATERIA
- PIZZA
- **Piazza Dante**
- Dante M
- GESÙ NUOVO
- Piazza Gesù Nuovo
- SAN DOM.
- SEBASTIANO
- VIA B. CROCE
- CHAPEL OF MARADONA
- PIZZA
- WALK ENDS
- To Piazza Garibaldi & Centrale station (10 min. walk)
- Piazza Sette Settembre
- "SPACCANAPOLI"
- SCATURCHIO PASTICCERIA
- MEZZOCANNONE
- VIA TOLEDO
- VIA MADDALONI
- **SANTA CHIARA**
- SANTA CHIARA
- CALATA TRINITA MAGGIORE
- CORSO UMBERTO I
- NUOVA MARINA
- **Piazza Carità**
- VIA MORG.
- VIA MONTEOLIVETO
- VIA C POST BATT.
- Piazza Bovio
- SPANISH QUARTER
- VIA DIAZ
- VIA MEDINA
- VIA AGOSTINO DEPRETIS
- VIA ALCIDE D. GASPERI
- VIA CRISTOFORO COLOMBO
- BANCA INTESA SANPAOLO
- *Port*
- VIA TOLEDO
- **GALLERIA UMBERTO I**
- Centrale Funicular
- Alibus Bus To Airport
- B
- Piazza Municipio
- B Bus to Train Station
- STAZIONE MARITTIMA
- GRAN CAFFÈ GAMBRINUS
- TEATRO DI SAN CARLO
- CASTEL NUOVO
- PORT BEVERELLO (BOATS TO SORRENTO & CAPRI)
- **ROYAL PALACE**
- Piazza del Plebiscito
- V. AM. FERDINANDO ACTON
- S. FRANCESCO DI PAOLA
- CONSOLE
- TUNNEL
- VIA NAZARIO SAURO
- *Bay of Naples*
- To Castel dell'Ovo
- 300 Meters
- 300 Yards

Dante—see his statue in the distance.

Piazza Dante: This square is marked by a statue of Dante, the medieval poet. Here you can feel Italy...but many Neapolitans merely feel the repression of the central state. When Napoleon was defeated, Naples became its own independent kingdom. But with Italian unification in 1861, Naples went from being a thriving cultural and political capital to a provincial town, its money used to help establish the industrial strength of the north. Originally, a statue of a Spanish Bourbon king stood here. The grand red-and-gray building is typical of Bourbon structures from that period. With the unification of Italy, the king, symbolic of Italy's colonial subjugation, was replaced by Dante—considered the father of the Italian language and a strong symbol of nationalism.

Old Dante looks out over an urban area that was once grand, then chaotic, and is now slowly becoming grand again. Behind Dante's right shoulder is the Port'Alba, part of Naples' old wall and the entrance to a small street lined with book vendors. Via Pessina, the long, straight street that you're walking, originated as a military road built by Spain in the 16th century. It skirted the old town wall to connect the Spanish military headquarters (now the museum) with the Royal Palace (down by the bay). A subway station called Dante (with a modern-art flair) was recently built here on Piazza Dante. Construction was slowed by the city's rich underground history: 13 feet down—Roman ruins; 23 feet down—Greek ruins; and every inch of the way—big headaches for construction workers.

Across the street, **Caffè Mexico** (at #86) is an institution known for its espresso, which is served already sweetened—ask for *senza zucchero* if you don't want sugar (pay first, then take receipt to the counter; locals tip €0.10). Most Italians agree that Neapolitan coffee is the best anywhere.

Continue walking downhill, remembering that here in Naples, red lights are considered "decorations." When crossing a street, try to tag along with a native. The people here are survivors: A long history of corrupt and greedy colonial overlords has taught Neapolitans to deal creatively with authority. Many credit this aspect of Naples' past for the advent of organized crime here.

Via Pessina becomes Via Toledo (another reminder of Spanish rule), Naples' principal shopping street. In 1860, from the white marble balcony of the Neoclassical building overlooking Piazza Sette Settembre, the famous revolutionary Giuseppe Garibaldi declared Italy united and Victor Emmanuel II its first king. Not until 1870, when Rome fell to the unification forces, was the dream of Italian unity fully realized.

• *Continue straight on Via Toledo. About three blocks below Piazza Dante and a block past Piazza Sette Settembre, you'll come to the long, straight, and narrow street called...*

Spaccanapoli: Before crossing the street—whose name translates as "split Naples"—look left. Look right. Since ancient times, this thin street has bisected the city. It changes names several times: Maddaloni (as it's called here), Via B. Croce, Via S. Biagio dei Librai, Forcella, and Vicaria. We'll return to this intersection later. (If you want to abbreviate this walk, turn left here and skip ahead to "Part 2.")

• *Stay on Via Toledo, which runs through...*

Piazza Carità: Surrounded by fascist architecture from 1938, this square is full of stern, straight, obedient lines. (For the best fascist architecture in town, take a slight detour from here—with your back to Via Toledo, leave Piazza Carità downhill on the right-hand corner and walk a block to the Poste e Telegrafi building. There you'll see several government buildings with stirring reliefs singing the praises of a totalitarian society.)

• *From Piazza Carità, continue south down Via Toledo for a few blocks, looking to your left for more examples of...*

Fascist Architecture (Banks): Notice the two banks. Try robbing the Banco di Napoli (Via Toledo 178). Step across the street and check out its architecture: typical fascist arches and reliefs, built to celebrate the bank's 400th anniversary (est. 1539—how old is *your* bank?).

On the next corner, **Banca Intesa Sanpaolo** fills an older palace—take a free peek at the opulent interior. On the second floor is a great late Caravaggio painting. *The Martyrdom of Saint Ursula* shows a terrible scene: His marriage proposal rejected, the king of the Huns flings an arrow into Ursula's chest. Blood spurts, Ursula is stunned but accepts her destiny sweetly, and Caravaggio himself—far right, his last self-portrait—screams to symbolize the rejection of evil (€4, Tue-Sun 10:00-18:00, closed Mon; includes 40-minute audioguide, a look at old Naples paintings, and a fine WC; www.palazzozevallos.com).

• *Feeling bold? From here, side-trip uphill a couple of blocks into the...*

Spanish Quarter: This is a classic world of *basso* (low) living. In such tight quarters, families generally do it in the road. This is *the* cliché of life in Naples, as shown in so many movies. The Spanish Quarter is Naples at its rawest, poorest, and most characteristic. The only predictable things about this Neapolitan tide pool are the ancient grid plan of its streets (which survives from Greek times), the friendliness of its shopkeepers, and the boldness

of its mopeds. Concerned locals will tug on their lower eyelids, warning you to be wary. Hungry? Pop into a grocery shop and ask the man to make you his best prosciutto and mozzarella sandwich (the price should be about €4).

• *Return to Via Toledo (clogged with more people than cars) and work your way down to the immense...*

Piazza del Plebiscito: This square celebrates the 1861 vote (*plebiscito*, plebiscite), when Naples chose to join Italy. Walk to the middle of the square. From here, you'll see the Church of San Francesco di Paola, with its Pantheon-inspired dome and broad, arcing colonnades.

• *Opposite is the...*

Royal Palace *(Palazzo Reale)*: Having housed Spanish, French, and even Italian royalty, this building displays statues of all those who stayed here. Look for eight kings in the niches, each from a different dynasty (left to right): Norman, German, French, Spanish, Spanish, Spanish, French (Napoleon's brother-in-law), and, finally, Italian—Victor Emmanuel II, King of Savoy. The statues were done at the request of V. E. II's son, so his dad is the most dashing of the group. This huge, lavish palace welcomes the public (€4, more with special exhibits, Thu-Tue 9:00-20:00, closed Wed, last entry one hour before closing, audioguide-€4, tel. 848-800-288).

The palace's grand Neoclassical staircase leads up to a floor with 30 plush rooms. You'll follow a one-way route (with some English descriptions) featuring paintings by "the Caravaggio Imitators," Neapolitan tapestries, fine inlaid-stone tabletops, and more. Don't miss the huge Hercules room and the chapel with a fantastic nativity scene (a commotion of 18th-century ceramic figurines).

The **Gran Caffè Gambrinus,** facing the piazza, takes you back to the elegance of 1860. It's a classic place to sample a unique Neapolitan treat called *sfogliatella* (crispy scallop shell-shaped pastry filled with sweet ricotta cheese). Or you might prefer the mushroom-shaped, rum-soaked bread-like cakes called *babà*, which come in a huge variety. Stand at the bar *(banco)*, pay double to sit *(tavola)*, or just wander around as you imagine the café buzzing with the ritzy intellectuals, journalists, and artsy bohemian types who munched on *babà* here during Naples' 19th-century heyday (daily 7:00-24:00, Piazza del Plebiscito 1, tel. 081-417-582).

• *Continue 50 yards past the Royal Palace (toward the trees) to enjoy a...*

Fine Harbor View: While boats busily serve Capri and Sorrento, Mount Vesuvius smolders ominously in the distance. Look back to see the vast "Bourbon red" palace—its color inspired by Pompeii. On the hilltop above Piazza del Plebiscito is Naples' Carthusian Monastery and the Castle of St. Elmo. This street continues to Naples' romantic harborfront—the fishermen's quarters (Borgo Marinaro)—a fortified island connected to the mainland by a stout causeway, with its fanciful Castel dell'Ovo (castle of the egg) and trendy harborside restaurants. Farther along the harborfront stretches the Lungomare promenade and Santa Lucia district. (The long harborfront promenade, Via Francesco Caracciolo, is a delightful people-watching scene on balmy nights.)

• *Head back to the piazza and go behind the palace, where you can peek inside the Neoclassical...*

Teatro di San Carlo: Built in 1737, 41 years before Milan's La Scala, this is Europe's oldest opera house and Italy's second-most-respected (after La Scala). The theater burned down in 1816, and was rebuilt within the year. Guided 35-minute visits basically just show you the fine auditorium with its 184 boxes—each with a big mirror to reflect the candlelight (€5, Mon-Sat 10:00-17:30, tours every 40 minutes, closed Sun, tel. 081-553-4565, www.teatrosancarlo.it).

Beyond Teatro di San Carlo and the Royal Palace is the huge, harborfront Castel Nuovo, which houses government bureaucrats and the **Civic Museum,** featuring 14th- to 16th-century art (€5, Mon-Sat 9:00-19:00, closed Sun, last entry one hour before closing, tel. 081-795-5877).

Across the street from Teatro di San Carlo, go through the tall yellow arch into the Victorian iron and glass of the 100-year-old shopping mall, **Galleria Umberto I.** Gawk up.

• *For Part 2 of this walk, double back up Via Toledo to Piazza Carità, veering right on Via Morgantini through Piazza Monteoliveto to the fancy column at the top of the hill. (To avoid the backtracking and uphill walk, catch a €10 taxi to the Church of Gesù Nuovo—JAY-zoo noo-OH-voh.)*

Part 2: Spaccanapoli Back to the Station

You're back at the straight-as-a-Greek-arrow Spaccanapoli, formerly the main thoroughfare of the Greek city of Neapolis.

• *Stop at...*

Piazza Gesù Nuovo: This square is marked by a towering 18th-century Baroque monument to the Counter-Reformation.

Although the Jesuit order was powerful in Naples because of its Spanish heritage, locals never attacked Protestants here with the full fury of the Spanish Inquisition. The square also has a handy little TI and is the starting point for electric bus #E1, which makes a 40-minute loop through the characteristic old quarter and ends up back here (€1.20, buy ticket at nearby newsstand before boarding, 2/hour, daily 7:00-24:00).

• *Now visit two bulky old churches, starting with the austere, fortress-like 17th-century...*

Church of Gesù Nuovo: The unique pyramid-grill facade survives from a fortified 15th-century noble palace. Step inside for a brilliant Neapolitan Baroque interior. The second chapel on the right features a much-adored statue of Giuseppe Moscati (1880-1927), a Christian doctor famous for helping the poor. In 1987, Moscati became the first modern doctor to be canonized.

Continue on to the third chapel and enter the **Sale Moscati.** This huge room is filled with "Ex Votos"—tiny red-and-silver plaques of thanksgiving for prayers answered with the help of St. Moscati (each has a symbol of the ailment cured). Naples' practice of using Ex Votos, while incorporated into its Catholic rituals, goes back to its pagan Greek roots. Rooms from Moscati's nearby apartment are on display, and a glass case shows possessions and photos of the great doctor. As you leave the Sale Moscati, notice the big bomb casing that hangs in the left corner. It fell through the church's dome in 1943, but caused almost no damage...yet another miracle (daily 7:00-13:00 & 16:00-19:30).

• *Head across the street, to the simpler...*

Church of Santa Chiara: Dating from the 14th century, this church is from a period of French royal rule under the Angevin dynasty. Consider the stark contrast between this church (Gothic) and the Gesù Nuovo (Baroque). Notice the huge inlaid-marble Angevin coat of arms on the floor. The faded Trinity on the back wall, to the left of the entry, shows a dove representing the Holy Spirit between the heads of God the Father and Christ (c. 1414). This is an example of the fine frescoes that once covered the walls. Most were stuccoed over during Baroque times or destroyed in 1943 by World War II bombs. The altar is adorned with four finely carved Gothic tombs of Angevin kings. A chapel stacked with Bourbon royalty is just to the right (daily 7:00-13:00 & 16:30-20:00).

• *Leaving the church, take a right and head to the back of the building. Continue through the archway straight ahead, and pass all the parked cars to reach the farthest door on the right. Here you'll find the bright, ornate majolica-tiled...*

Cloistered Courtyard of Santa Chiara: Note the sprawling nativity scene immediately on your right as you enter—a cartoonish

3-D snapshot of Old World Napoli. Stop in at its museum for a peek at the excavations of an ancient bath complex (€5, Mon-Sat 9:30-17:30, Sun 10:00-14:30, last entry 30 minutes before closing, tel. 081-551-6673, www.monasterodisantachiara.eu).

• *Now return to the main drag, turn right, and continue straight down traffic-free Via B. Croce. A good little lunch spot,* **Trattoria da Titina e Gennaro,** *is just down the street across from the church (Via Santa Chiara 6).*

Since this is a university district, you'll see lots of students and bookstores. This neighborhood is also extremely superstitious. Look for incense-burning women with carts full of good-luck charms for sale.

• *Farther down Spaccanapoli, you'll see the next square...*

Piazza San Domenico Maggiore: This square is marked by an ornate 17th-century monument built to thank God for ending the plague. But more important is the well-loved **Scaturchio Pasticceria,** another good place to try *sfogliatella* (€1.50 to go, costs double at a table in the square, daily 7:20-20:40, tel. 081-551-7031).

• *From this square, detour left along the right side of the castle-like church, then follow yellow signs, taking the first right and walking one block to...*

Cappella Sansevero: This small chapel is a Baroque explosion mourning the body of Christ, who lies on a soft pillow under an incredibly realistic veil. It's also the personal chapel of Raimondo de Sangro, an eccentric Freemason. The monuments to his relatives have a second purpose: to share the Freemason philosophy of freedom through enlightenment (€7, Mon and Wed-Sat 10:00-18:00, Sun 10:00-13:30, closed Tue, last entry 20 minutes before closing, no photos but postcards sold in gift shop, Via de Sanctis 19, tel. 081-551-8470).

Study the incredible *Veiled Christ* in the center. Carved out of marble, it's like no other statue I've seen (by Giuseppe "Howdeedoodat" Sammartino, 1753). The Christian message (Jesus died for our salvation) is accompanied by a Freemason message (the veil represents how the body and ego are obstacles to real spiritual freedom). As you walk from Christ's feet to his head, notice how the expression on Jesus' face goes from suffering to peace.

Raimondo de Sangro lies buried at the far (altar) end. An inventor, he created the deep-green pigment used on the ceiling fresco. The inlaid M. C. Escher-esque maze on the floor around de Sangro's tomb is another Freemason reminder of how the quest for knowledge gets you out of the maze of life.

To the right of the altar, the statue *Despair* struggles with a marble rope net (carved out of a single piece of stone), symbolic of a troubled mind. The Freemason symbolism shows how knowledge—in the guise of an angel—frees the human mind. On the opposite side of the altar from *Despair,* a veiled woman fingers a broken plaque, symbolizing...something.

Your Sansevero finale is downstairs: two mysterious...skeletons. Perhaps another of the mad inventor's fancies: Inject a corpse with a fluid to fossilize the veins so that they'll survive the body's decomposition. While that's the legend, it was most likely created to illustrate how the circulatory system works.

• *Return to Via B. Croce (a.k.a. Spaccanapoli), turn left, and continue your cultural scavenger hunt. At the intersection of Via Nilo, find the...*

Statue of the Nile (on the left): A reminder of the multiethnic make-up of Greek Neapolis, this statue is in what was the Egyptian quarter. Locals like to call this statue *The Body of Naples,* with the overflowing cornucopia symbolizing the abundance of their fine city. (I once asked a Neapolitan man to describe the local women, who are famous for their beauty, in one word. He replied simply, "Abundant.") This intersection is considered the center of old Naples.

• *Directly opposite the statue is the...*

"Chapel of Maradona": The niche on the wall is dedicated to Diego Maradona, a soccer star who played for Naples in the 1980s. Locals consider soccer almost a religion, and this guy was practically a deity. You can even see a "hair of Diego" and a teardrop from the city when he went to another team for more money. Unfortunately, his reputation has since been sullied by problems he's had with organized crime, drugs, and police.

A few blocks farther along Spaccanapoli, at the tiny square, Via San Gregorio Armeno leads left into a colorful district (and also to the underground Napoli Sotterranea archaeological site). You'll see many shops that sell tiny components of fantastic *presepi* (nativity scenes), including figurines caricaturing local politicians and celebrities. Just as many Americans keep an eye out year-round for Christmas-tree ornaments, Italians regularly add pieces to the family *presepe,* the centerpiece of their holiday celebrations.

• *Back on Spaccanapoli, as Via B. Croce becomes Via S. Biagio dei Librai, notice the...*

Gold and Silver Shops: Some say stolen jewelry ends up here, is melted down immediately, and gets resold in some other form as soon as it cools. The inimitable Sr. Grassi runs the Ospedale delle Bambole (doll hospital) at #81.

• *Cross busy Via Duomo.*

Here, the street and side-street scenes along Via Vicaria intensify. This is known as a center of the Camorra (organized crime).

Paint a picture with these thoughts: Naples has the most intact street plan of any ancient Roman city. Imagine this city during those times (and retain these images as you visit Pompeii), with streetside shop fronts that close up after dark, turning into private

NAPLES

homes. Today, it's just one more page in a 2,000-year-old story of a city: all kinds of meetings, beatings, and cheatings; kisses, near misses, and little-boy pisses.

You name it, it occurs right on the streets today, as it has since ancient times. People ooze from crusty corners. Black-and-white death announcements add to the clutter on the walls. Widows sell cigarettes from buckets. For a peek behind the scenes in the shade of wet laundry, venture down a few side streets. Buy two carrots as a gift for the woman on the fifth floor if she'll lower her bucket to pick them up. The

neighborhood action seems best at about 18:00.

A few blocks on, at the tiny fenced-in triangle of greenery, hang out for a few minutes to just observe the crazy motorbike action and teen scene.

• *From here, veer right onto Via Forcella (which leads to the busy boulevard that takes you to the Centrale station). A block down, a tiny, fenced-in traffic island protects a chunk of the ancient Greek wall of Neapolis (fourth century B.C.). Turn right here on Via Pietro Colletta, walk 40 yards, and step into the North Pole, at the...*

Polo Nord Gelateria: The oldest *gelateria* in Naples has had four generations of family working here since 1931. Before you order, sample a few flavors, including their *bacio* or "kiss" flavor (chocolate and hazelnut)—all are made fresh daily (Mon-Sat 10:00-23:00, Sun 10:00-14:00 & 17:00-23:00, Via Pietro Colletta 41, tel. 081-205-431). Via Pietro Colletta leads past Napoli's two most competitive **pizzerias** (see "Eating in Naples," later) to Corso Umberto I.

• *Turn left on the grand boulevard-like Corso Umberto I. From here to the Centrale station, it's at least a 10-minute walk (if you're tired, hop on a bus; they all go to the station). To finish the walk, continue on Corso Umberto I—past a gauntlet of purse/CD/sunglasses salesmen and shady characters hawking stolen camcorders—to the vast, ugly Piazza Garibaldi. On the far side is the station. You made it.*

More Sights in Naples

▲▲**Napoli Sotterranea**—This archaeological site, a manmade underground maze of passageways and ruins from Greek and Roman times, can only be toured with a guide. You'll descend 121 steps under the modern city to explore. The first stop is the old Greek tuff quarry used to build the city of Neapolis, which was later converted into an immense aqueduct by the Romans.

Next is an excavated portion of the Greco-Roman theater. The tour involves a lot of stairs, as well as a long, narrow 20-inch-wide walkway that uses an ancient water channel (a heavyset person could not comfortably fit through this). Although there's not much to actually see, the experience is fascinating, and includes a little WWII history.

Cost and Hours: €9.30; includes 1.5-hour tour. Visits in English are offered daily at 12:00, 14:00, and 16:00; also at 10:00 and 18:00 Sat-Sun. Bring a light sweater. Tel. 081-296-944, www.napolisotterranea.org.

The site is a 10-minute walk from the Archaeological Museum, just west of Via Duomo, next to the church of San Paolo off Via dei Tribunali, at Piazza Gaetano 68. From Spaccanapoli, it's just a couple blocks uphill from the Statue of the Nile (ask for Piazza Gaetano, and look for the *Sotterranea* signs).

Open-Air Fish Market—Naples' fish market squirts and stinks as it has for centuries under the Porta Nolana (gate in the city wall) just four blocks from the Centrale station. Of the town's many

boisterous outdoor markets, this will net you the most photos and memories. From Piazza Nolana, wander under the medieval gate and take your first left down Vico Sopramuro, enjoying this wild and entirely edible cultural scavenger hunt (Tue-Sun 8:00-14:00, closed Mon).

Two other markets with more clothing and less fish are at Piazza Capuana (several blocks northwest of the Centrale station and tumbling down Via Sant'Antonio Abate, Mon-Sat 8:00-18:00, Sun 9:00-13:00) and a similar cobbled shopping zone along Via Pignasecca (just off Via Toledo, west of Piazza Carità).

Grand View from Certosa San Martino—This ultimate view overlooking Naples, its bay, and a volcano comes with a €6 price tag. The monastery, founded in 1325 and dissolved in the early 1800s, is popular today for its dramatic view gardens, church, and museum, which features a history of the kingdoms of southern Italy and the city's best collection of *presepi* manger scenes (Thu-Tue 8:30-19:30, closed Wed, last entry 1.5 hours before closing, Metro: Montesanto, well-posted 10-minute walk from top of Montesanto funicular at Largo San Martino 5, tel. 081-558-6408).

Lungomare *Passeggiata*—Each evening, relaxed and romantic Neapolitans in the mood for a scenic harborside stroll do their *vasche* (laps) along the inviting Lungomare promenade. To join in this elegant people-watching scene (best after 19:00), stroll about

NAPLES

15 minutes from Piazza del Plebiscito along Via Nazario Sauro.

Detour out along the fortified causeway to poke around Borgo Marinaro ("fishermen's quarters"), with its striking Castel dell'Ovo and a trendy restaurant scene where you can dine amidst yachts with a view of Vesuvius. This is known as the Santa Lucia district because this is where the song "Santa Lucia" was first performed. (The song is probably so famous in America because immigrants from Naples sang it to remember the old country.) Beyond that stretches the Lungomare, along Via Francesco Caracciolo. Taxi home or retrace your steps back to the old center.

Sleeping in Naples

With Sorrento just an hour away (see next chapter), I can't imagine why you'd sleep in Naples. But, if needed, here are a few options. The last three are within a few blocks of the train station, but be forewarned: The area can feel unnerving, especially after dark. In this business-oriented (rather than tourist-oriented) city, summer (July-Sept) is low season, when prices are particularly soft.

$$ Pinto-Storey Hotel seems a world away from the bustle of the rest of the city. In an upscale neighborhood (three Metro stops from the train station), its 16 charming rooms feel as fresh as when the hotel opened—in 1878 (Sb-€78, Db-€98, Tb-€139, these prices if you book direct and mention this book, air-con-€9, elevator, across the square from Metro line 2's Amedeo stop at Via Martucci 72, tel. 081-681-260, fax 081-667-536, www.pintostorey.it, info@pintostorey.it).

Near the Train Station: **$$ Grand Hotel Europa,** a gem set in the seedy neighborhood around the station, has 89 decent rooms

---

Sleep Code

(€1 = about $1.40, country code: 39)

S = Single, **D** = Double/Twin, **T** = Triple, **Q** = Quad, **b** = bathroom, **s** = shower only. Unless otherwise noted, credit cards are accepted, English is spoken, and breakfast is included.

To help you sort easily through these listings, I've divided the accommodations into three categories based on the price for a standard double room with bath:

$$ Higher Priced—Most rooms more than €80.
$ Lower Priced—Most rooms €80 or less.

Prices can change without notice; verify the hotel's current rates online or by email. For other updates, see www.ricksteves.com/update.

decorated with not-quite-right reproductions of famous paintings (Sb-€65, Db-€85, Tb-€109, book direct and ask for 15 percent Rick Steves discount off these prices or check website for special deals, air-con, Internet access, restaurant; from the station, walk 30 yards past track 5, turn left, make a quick right around the green *Polfer* sign, and go out the gate to Corso Meridionale 14; tel. 081-267-511, www.grandhoteleuropa.com, info@grandhoteleuropa.com, well-run by Claudio).

$$ Hotel Suite Esedra, with 19 small-but-tasteful rooms, is a four-star charmer on a tiny square off busy Corso Umberto I, located just outside of the station-neighborhood sleaze (Sb-€60, Db-€75-90, these prices if you book direct and mention this book, air-con, elevator, Wi-Fi, 10-minute walk from the station at Via Arnaldo Cantani 12, tel. 081-287-451, fax 081-553-7087, www.hotelsuiteesedranapoli.it, info@hotelsuiteesedranapoli.it, Alessandro).

$ Hotel Potenza offers 26 rooms, along with a rare bit of security and peace on Piazza Garibaldi (Sb-€55, Db-€75, air-con, no elevator, 100 yards in front of the station at Piazza Garibaldi 120, tel. 081-286-330, www.hotelpotenza.com, info@hotelpotenza .com, Valenzano family).

Eating in Naples

Cheap and Famous Pizza

Naples—whose pizzerias bake just the right combination of fresh dough, mozzarella, and tomatoes in traditional wood-burning ovens—is the birthplace of pizza. Drop by one of the two most venerable pizzerias in town (both a few long blocks from the station, at the end of my "A Slice of Neapolitan Life" self-guided walk).

Antica Pizzeria da Michele is for pizza purists. Filled with locals (and tourists), it serves just two varieties: *margherita* (tomato sauce and mozzarella) and *marinara* (tomato sauce, oregano, and garlic, no cheese). Come early to sit and watch the pizza artists in action. A pizza with beer costs €6 (Mon-Sat 10:30-24:00, closed Sun; look for the vertical red *Antica Pizzeria* sign at the intersection of Via Pietro Colletta and Via Cesare Sersale at #1; tel. 081-553-9204).

Pizzeria Trianon, across the street, has been da Michele's archrival since 1923. It offers more choices, slightly higher prices (€5-7), air-conditioning, and a cozier atmosphere. For less chaos, head upstairs. While waiting for your meal, you can survey the transformation of a humble wad of dough into a smoldering bubbly feast in their entryway pizza kitchen (daily 11:00-15:30 & 19:00-23:00, Via Pietro Colletta 42, tel. 081-553-9426, Giuseppe).

Getting Around the Region

To connect Naples, Sorrento, and the Amalfi Coast, you can travel on land by train, bus, and taxi. Whenever possible, consider taking a boat—it's faster, cooler, and more scenic, and you can take coastline photos that you can't get from land. For specific travel times and costs, check the "Connections" sections of the Naples, Sorrento, and Amalfi Coast chapters. It's always a good idea to confirm schedules and prices with the TI or your hotel.

By Circumvesuviana Train: This useful commuter train—popular with locals, tourists, and pickpockets—links Naples, Herculaneum, Pompeii, and Sorrento. At Naples' Centrale train station, follow the signs to the Circumvesuviana (across from track 13, downstairs, and down the corridor to the left), where you'll find the ticket office and info booth. When you buy your ticket, ask which track your train will depart from (**"Quale binario?"**; KWAH-lay bee-NAH-ree-oh). Just beyond, you'll find the gate where you insert your ticket. The train platforms are downstairs. The Circumvesuviana also has its own terminal (one Metro stop or a 10-minute walk beyond the Centrale station), but there's no reason to use it unless you're nearby.

Trains marked *Sorrento,* which depart twice hourly, take you to Herculaneum/Ercolano (about 25 minutes, €2.10 one-way), Pompeii (about 35 minutes, €2.80 one-way), and Sorrento, the end of the line (70 minutes, €4 one-way). There's no round-trip discount, and all-day passes are generally not worthwhile, except on weekends when they're roughly half-price. Though not covered by railpasses, Circumvesuviana tickets are covered by the Campania ArteCard (see page 4). Not all of the trains go as far as Sorrento; check the schedule or confirm with a local before boarding to make sure the train goes where you want. Express trains marked *DD* (6/day) get you to Sorrento 20 minutes sooner (and also stop at Herculaneum and Pompeii). When returning to Naples' Centrale station on the Circumvesuviana, get off at Garibaldi—the next-to-the-last stop (the Centrale station is just up the escalator). Bonus: When returning from Sorrento to Naples, you can use your Circumvesuviana ticket to cover Metro and bus rides within three hours of validation (no need to validate again). Be on guard: Though I haven't had problems, many readers report being ripped off on the Circumvesuviana (see "Theft Alert," page 5). For information, see www.vesuviana.it.

If you're coming **from Rome,** note that a different (non-Circumvesuviana) train—run by the national rail company—goes from Rome to Naples, then continues to the ugly modern city of Pompei. There is almost no reason to go to Pompei city, where you'll face a long walk to the actual site. Therefore, from Rome, it's better to simply get off at Naples' Centrale station and transfer to the Circumvesuviana (to the Pompei Scavi stop). The Pompei city train station is useful only for connecting to Salerno or Paestum (not quite hourly, 30 minutes to Salerno, 1 hour to Paestum, direction: Sapri).

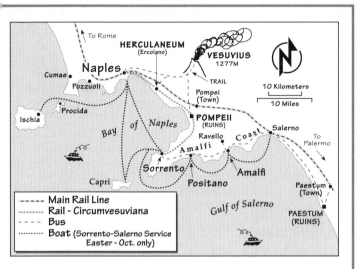

By Bus: SITA buses (often blue or green-and-white) connect the towns. Buses that travel along the highly touristed Amalfi Coast can be crowded; for tips, see "Getting Around the Amalfi Coast—By Bus" on page 84.

By Taxi: For €100, you can take a 30-mile taxi ride from Naples directly to your Sorrento hotel; agree on a set price without the meter and pay upon arrival. You can hire a cab on Capri for about €70/hour. Taxis in the Amalfi Coast are generally expensive, and more than willing to overcharge you, but they can be convenient, especially with a larger group. See "Getting Around the Amalfi Coast—By Taxi" on page 85.

By Boat: Several primary ferry companies service the Naples, Sorrento, and Amalfi Coast areas: Caremar (www.caremar.it), SNAV (www.snav.it), Gescab (www.gescab.it), and TravelMar (www.travelmar.it). Each company has different destinations and prices; some compete for the same trips. The quicker the trip, the higher the price. A hydrofoil, called a "jet boat," skims between Naples and Sorrento—it's faster, safer from pickpockets, more scenic, and more expensive than the Circumvesuviana train (6/day, more in summer, departs roughly every 2 hours starting at 9:00, 35 minutes, €10). A taxi from Naples' Centrale train station to its port costs about €12-15.

For schedules to Capri, you can check online (www.capri tourism.com; click "Shipping Timetable"), at any TI, or at the Port Beverello boat dock. Ticket windows clearly display the next available departure. The number of boats that run per day depends on the season. Trips are canceled in bad weather. Most boats charge an extra fee for luggage (about €2).

If you plan to arrive at and leave a destination by boat, make note upon your arrival of the return times—the last boat usually leaves before 19:00.

Near the Archaeological Museum

Caffetteria Angela is a fun little eating complex: coffee bar; *tavola calda* with hot ready-to-eat dishes (€3-4); and a tiny meat, cheese, and bread shop with all you need for a cheap meal to go. It offers honest pricing and simple, peaceful, air-conditioned indoor seating (no cover, open Mon-Sat 7:00-21:00, Sun 9:00-14:00, just off Via Pessina, 3 blocks below museum at Via Conte di Ruvo 21, tel. 081-549-9660).

Salumeria Pasquale Carrino is a tiny salami shop with an exuberant owner—the fun-loving and flamboyant Pasquale—who turns sandwich-making into a show (€6 sandwich good for two people, Mon-Sat 8:00-15:00 & 16:30-20:00, closed Sun, 100 yards from museum—as you leave take two rights and a left to Via Salvator Rosa 10, tel. 081-564-0889).

Near the Station

La Cantina dei Mille, a block in front of the train station, is a traditional family-style place serving good, basic Neapolitan food to good, basic Neapolitans indoors and out. It's about the only charming place I found on Piazza Garibaldi (€5 pizza and pasta, daily 12:00-16:00 & 17:00-24:00; with your back to the station, it's about halfway up the left side of Piazza Garibaldi at #126; tel. 081-283-448).

Next door, **Iris'** cadre of bow-tied waiters sling good, reasonably priced seafood, pastas, and pizzas in a comfortable *ristorante* with an outdoor patio (Sun-Fri 12:00-15:30 & 18:30-23:00, closed Sat, Piazza Garibaldi 121, tel. 081-269-988).

Grand Hotel Europa (see "Sleeping in Naples," earlier) has a restaurant peacefully buried in its basement, offering friendly service and a fine value (daily, light lunches anytime, dinner 19:00-23:00).

Naples Connections

From Naples by Boat to: Sorrento (6/day, more in summer, leaves roughly every 2 hours starting at 9:00, 35 minutes, €10), **Capri** (roughly 2/hour, 45 minutes, €16). Seasonal boats to **Positano** (June-Oct only, 4/day, 1.25-1.5 hours, €14.50) continue on to **Amalfi** (1.5-2 hours, €15).

By Train to: Rome (at least hourly, 1.25 hours on Frecciarossa express trains, otherwise 2-2.5 hours), **Florence** (hourly, 3-5 hours, some change in Rome), **Salerno** (2/hour, 45-75 minutes, avoid slow *diretto* train), **Paestum** (almost hourly, 1.5 hours, direction: Sapri), **Brindisi** (8/day, 5-8 hours, overnight possible; from Brindisi, ferries sail to Greece), **Milan** (direct trains hourly, 5 hours, more with change in Rome, overnight possible), **Venice** (almost hourly,

5.5-7 hours with changes in Bologna or Rome, overnight possible), **Palermo** (3/day, 10 hours, overnight possible), **Nice** (2/day, 12 hours with change in Genoa), **Paris** (3/day, 13-15 hours with change in Rome or Milan). Any train listed on the schedule as leaving Napoli PG or Napoli-Garibaldi departs not from the actual station, but from the Piazza Garibaldi subway station below.

To Pompeii: To visit the ancient site of Pompeii, don't use national train connections to the city of Pompei (which might seem convenient, especially if you're coming from Rome). Because the Pompei national train station is far from the archaeological site, you're better off transferring in Naples to the Circumvesuviana train (below)—which takes you to the Pompei Scavi stop near the actual site.

By Circumvesuviana Train: See "Getting Around the Region" sidebar, earlier, for information on getting to Herculaneum, Pompeii, and Sorrento.

NAPLES

Pompeii, Herculaneum, and Vesuvius

Stopped in their tracks by the eruption of Mount Vesuvius in A.D. 79, Pompeii and Herculaneum offer the best look anywhere at what life in Rome must have been like around 2,000 years ago. These two cities of well-preserved ruins are yours to explore. Of the two sites, Pompeii is grander, while Herculaneum is smaller and more intimate. Vesuvius, still smoldering ominously, rises up on the horizon. It last erupted in 1944, and is still an active volcano. Buses drop you a steep half-hour hike from the summit.

Pompeii

A once-thriving commercial port of 20,000, Pompeii (worth ▲▲▲) grew from Greek and Etruscan roots to become an important Roman city. Then, on August 24, A.D. 79, everything changed. Vesuvius erupted and began to bury the city under 30 feet of hot volcanic ash. For the archaeologists who excavated it centuries later, this was a shake-and-bake windfall, teaching them volumes about daily Roman life. Pompeii was  accidentally rediscovered in 1599; excavations began in 1748.

Orientation to Pompeii

Cost: €11, €20 combo-ticket includes Herculaneum (called Ercolano) and three lesser sites (valid 3 consecutive days).

Hours: Daily April-Oct 8:30-19:30, Nov-March 8:30-17:00 (last entry 1.5 hours before closing).

Getting There: Pompeii is roughly midway between Naples and Sorrento on the Circumvesuviana train line (2/hour, €2.80 and 35 minutes from Naples, €2.10 and 30 minutes from Sorrento, one-way, not covered by railpasses, www.vesuviana.it). Get off at the Pompei Scavi, Villa dei Misteri stop; from Naples, it's the stop after Torre Annunziata; from Sorrento, it's the one after Moregine). The DD express trains bypass several of the suburban stations but stop at the site, making the trip slightly faster. You can store your bag at the train station's bar for a small fee (€2, confirm last pickup time—bar often closes early), or, better yet, use the free baggage check at the site. From the Pompei Scavi train station, turn right and walk down the road about a block to the entrance (first left turn). The TI is farther down the street, but it's not a necessary stop for your visit. Parking is available at Camping Zeus near the Circumvesuviana train station (€2.50/hour).

Information: A good map and a helpful information booklet (which describes the most important stops within the site), when available, are included with your admission, but you must pick them up at the information window (to the left of the WCs). Tel. 081-857-5347, www.pompeiisites.org.

The bookshop sells the small Pompeii and Herculaneum *Past and Present* book. Its helpful text and plastic overlays allow you to re-create the ruins (€12 in bookstores, pay no more than that if you buy from a street vendor; look for the current year's edition).

Be warned that some buildings and streets are bound to be closed for restoration when you visit.

Tours: My self-guided tour in this chapter covers the basics and provides a good framework for exploring the site on your own.

Live guides (around €115/2 hours) of varying quality—there really is no guarantee of what you're getting—cluster near the ticket booth and may try to herd you into a group with other travelers, which makes the price more reasonable for you. For a private tour, consider the knowledgeable **Gaetano Manfredi,** who brings energy, intensity, and theatricality to his tours. He's a joy to follow for two hours as he brings the dusty ruins to life. Avoid impersonators. The real Gaetano takes bookings only in advance, preferably by email (rates vary with season and group size, mobile 338-725-5620, www.pompeiitourguide.com, gaetanoguide@hotmail.it). **Antonio Somma** also specializes in the site and does tours of the surrounding region (book in advance, mobile 339-891-9489, www.pompeitour.com, info@pompeitour.com). Parents, note that the ancient brothel and its sexually explicit frescoes are included on tours; let your guide know if you'd rather skip that stop.

Audioguides are available from a kiosk near the ticket booth at the Porta Marina entrance (€6.50, €10/2 people, ID required), but they offer basically the same info as your free booklet.

Length of This Tour: Allow three hours.

Baggage Check: A free baggage check is near the turnstiles at the site entrance.

Visiting Vesuvius: If you want to visit Mount Vesuvius, you can take a bus from Pompeii (or from Herculaneum; for details, see "Vesuvius" at the end of this chapter).

Services: The site has two WCs—one near the entrance and another in the cafeteria.

NAPLES

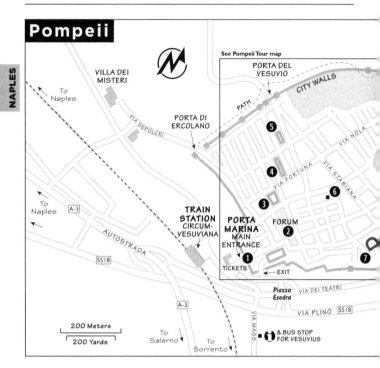

Pompeii

VILLA DEI MISTERI

To Naples

PORTA DEL VESUVIO

CITY WALLS

See Pompeii Tour map

VIA SEPOLCRI

PORTA DI ERCOLANO

PATH

5

4 VIA FORTUNA

VIA NOLA

VIA STABIANA

To Naples

A-3

3

6

AUTOSTRADA

TRAIN STATION CIRCUM-VESUVIANA

PORTA MARINA MAIN ENTRANCE

FORUM

2

SS18

1

TICKETS

← EXIT

Piazza Esedra VIA DEI TEATRI

7

A-3

VIA PLINO SS18

200 Meters

200 Yards

To Salerno

To Sorrento

VIA MASS

& BUS STOP FOR VESUVIUS

Cuisine Art: The restaurant within the site serves edible sandwiches, pizza, and pasta at a reasonable price. A few mediocre restaurants cluster between the entrance and the train station. Your best bet may be to bring your own food for a discreet picnic.

Starring: Roofless (collapsed) but otherwise intact Roman buildings, plaster casts of hapless victims, a few erotic frescoes, and the dawning realization that these ancient people were no different from us.

Background

Pompeii, founded in 600 B.C., eventually became a booming Roman trading city. Not rich, not poor, it was middle class—a perfect example of typical Roman life. Most streets would have been lined with stalls and jammed with customers from sunup to sundown. Chariots vied with shoppers for street space. Two thousand years ago, Rome controlled the entire Mediterranean—making it a kind of free-trade zone—and

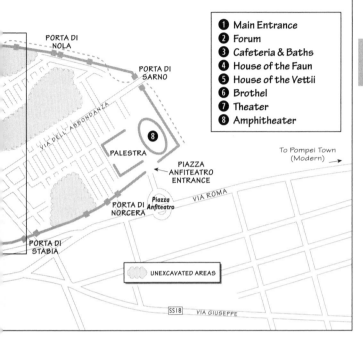

Pompeii was a central and bustling port.

There were no posh neighborhoods in Pompeii. Rich and poor mixed it up as elegant houses existed side by side with simple homes. While nearby Herculaneum would have been a classier place to live (traffic-free streets, fancier houses, far better drainage), Pompeii was the place for action and shopping. It served an estimated 20,000 residents with more than 40 bakeries, 30 brothels, and 130 bars, restaurants, and hotels. With most of its buildings covered by brilliant white ground-marble stucco, Pompeii in A.D. 79 was an impressive town.

As you tour Pompeii, remember that its best art is in the Archaeological Museum in Naples (described earlier in this chapter).

Self-Guided Tour

• *Just past the ticket-taker, start your approach up to the...*

❶ Porta Marina

The city of Pompeii was born on the hill ahead of you. This was the original town gate. Before Vesuvius blew and filled in the harbor, the sea came nearly to here. Look to the left (near the tall cypress

tree in the distance) to see the stone rings where ships tied up to the dock. Also notice the two openings in the gate (ahead, up the ramp). Both were left open by day to admit major traffic. At night, the larger one was closed for better security.

• *Pass through the Porta Marina and continue up to the top of the street, pausing at the three large stepping-stones in the middle.*

❷ Pompeii's Streets

Every day, Pompeiians flooded the streets with gushing water to clean them. These stepping-stones let pedestrians cross without get-

ting their sandals wet. Chariots traveling in either direction could straddle the stones (all had standard-size axles). A single stepping-stone in a road means it was a one-way street, a pair indicates an ordinary two-way, and three (like this) signifies a major thoroughfare. The basalt stones are the original Roman pavement. The sidewalks (elevated to hide the plumbing) were paved with bits of broken pots (an ancient form of recycling) and studded with reflective bits of white marble. These "cats' eyes" helped people get around after dark, either by moonlight or with the help of lamps.

• *Continue straight ahead, don your mental toga, and enter the city as the Romans once did. The road opens up into the spacious main square: the Forum. Stand at the near end of this rectangular space and look toward Mount Vesuvius.*

❸ The Forum (Foro)

Pompeii's commercial, religious, and political center stands at the intersection of the city's two main streets. While it's the most ruined part of Pompeii, it's grand nonetheless. Picture the piazza

surrounded by two-story buildings on all sides. The pedestals that line the square once held statues (now safely displayed in the museum in Naples). In its heyday, Pompeii's citizens gathered here in the main square to shop,

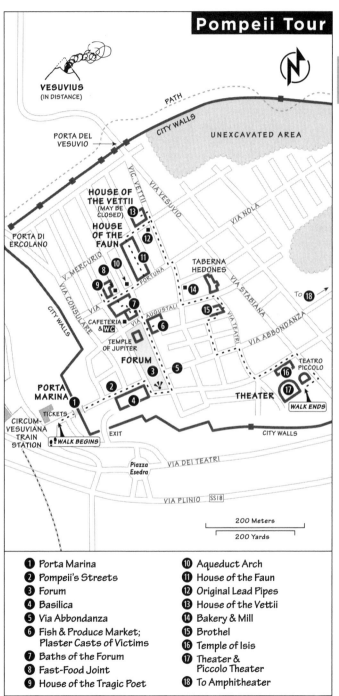

Pompeii Tour

VESUVIUS
(IN DISTANCE)

PATH

CITY WALLS

UNEXCAVATED AREA

PORTA DEL
VESUVIO

VIC. VETTII

VIA VESUVIO

VIA NOLA

HOUSE OF
THE VETTII
(MAY BE
CLOSED) **13**

HOUSE
OF THE
FAUN

PORTA DI
ERCOLANO

12

V. MERCURIO

11

TABERNA
HEDONES

VIA STABIANA

VIA
FORTUNA

8

10

VIA CONSULARE

9

14

To **18**

7

VIA
AUGUSTALI

VIA TEATRI

15

CITY WALLS

CAFETERIA
& **WC**

6

VIA ABBONDANZA

TEMPLE
OF JUPITER

FORUM

3

5

TEATRO
PICCOLO

16

PORTA
MARINA

2

4

17

THEATER

1

WALK ENDS

TICKETS

CIRCUM-
VESUVIANA
TRAIN
STATION

WALK BEGINS

EXIT

CITY WALLS

Piazza
Esedra

VIA DEI TEATRI

VIA PLINIO SS18

200 Meters

200 Yards

1 Porta Marina
2 Pompeii's Streets
3 Forum
4 Basilica
5 Via Abbondanza
6 Fish & Produce Market;
     Plaster Casts of Victims
7 Baths of the Forum
8 Fast-Food Joint
9 House of the Tragic Poet
10 Aqueduct Arch
11 House of the Faun
12 Original Lead Pipes
13 House of the Vettii
14 Bakery & Mill
15 Brothel
16 Temple of Isis
17 Theater &
     Piccolo Theater
18 To Amphitheater

talk politics, and socialize. Business took place in the important buildings that lined the piazza.

The Forum was dominated by the **Temple of Jupiter,** at the far end (marked by a half-dozen ruined columns atop a stair-step base). Jupiter was the supreme god of the Roman pantheon—you might be able to make out his little white marble head at the center-rear of the temple.

At the near end of the Forum (behind where you're standing) is the **curia,** or city hall. Like many Roman buildings, it was built with brick and mortar, then covered with marble walls and floors. To your left (as you face Vesuvius and the Temple of Jupiter) is the **basilica,** or courthouse.

Since Pompeii was a pretty typical Roman town, it has the same layout and components that you'll find in any Roman city—main square, curia, basilica, temples, axis of roads, and so on. All power converged at the Forum: religious (the temple), political (the curia), judicial (the basilica), and commercial (this piazza was the main marketplace). Even the power of the people was expressed here, since this where they gathered to vote. Imagine the hubbub of this town square in its heyday.

Look beyond the Temple of Jupiter. Five miles to the north looms the ominous backstory to this site: **Mount Vesuvius.** Mentally draw a triangle up from the two remaining peaks to reconstruct the mountain before the eruption. When it blew, Pompeiians had no idea that they were living under a volcano, since Vesuvius hadn't erupted for 1,200 years. Imagine the wonder—then the horror—as a column of pulverized rock roared upward, and then ash began to fall. The weight of the ash and small rocks collapsed Pompeii's roofs later that day, crushing people who had taken refuge inside buildings instead of fleeing the city.

• *As you face Vesuvius, the basilica is to your left, lined with stumps of columns. Step inside and see the layout.*

❹ Basilica

Pompeii's basilica was a first-century palace of justice. This ancient law court has the same floor plan later adopted by many Christian churches (which are also called basilicas). The big central hall (or nave) is flanked by rows of columns marking off narrower side aisles. Along the side walls are traces of the original marble.

The column stumps—all about the same height—were not ruined by the volcano. Rather, they were left unfinished when

The Eruption of Vesuvius

At about 1:00 in the afternoon on August 24, A.D. 79, Mount Vesuvius erupted, sending a mushroom cloud of ash, dust, and rocks 12 miles into the air. It spewed for 18 hours straight, as winds blew the cloud southward. The white-gray ash settled like a heavy snow on Pompeii, its weight eventually collapsing roofs and floors, but leaving the walls intact. While most of Pompeii's 20,000 residents fled that day, about two thousand stayed behind.

Although the city of Herculaneum was closer to the volcano—about four miles away—it had largely escaped the rain of ash, due to the direction of the wind. However, 12 hours after Vesuvius awoke, the type of eruption suddenly changed. The column of hot gas and rock collapsed, creating a superheated avalanche of ash, pumice, and gas. This red-hot "pyroclastic flow" sped down the side of the mountain at nearly 100 miles per hour, engulfing Herculaneum. Several more flows over the next few hours further entombed Herculaneum, burying it in nearly 60 feet of hot material that later cooled into rock, freezing the city in time. Then around 7:30 in the morning, another pyroclastic flow headed south and struck Pompeii, dealing a fatal blow to those who'd remained in that city.

Vesuvius blew. Pompeii had been devastated by an earthquake in A.D. 62, and was just in the process of rebuilding the basilica when Vesuvius erupted 17 years later. The half-built columns show off the technology of the day. Uniform bricks were stacked around a cylindrical core. Once finished, they would have been coated with marble dust stucco to simulate marble columns—an economical construction method found throughout Pompeii (and the Roman Empire).

Besides the earthquake and the eruption, Pompeii's buildings have suffered other ravages over the years, including Spanish plunderers (c. 1800), 19th-century souvenir hunters, WWII bombs, wild vegetation, and another earthquake in 1980. The fact that the entire city was covered by the eruption of A.D. 79 actually helped preserve it, saving it from the sixth-century barbarians who plundered many other towns into oblivion.

• *Exit the basilica and cross the short side of the square, where the city's main street hits the Forum.*

❺ Via Abbondanza

Look down Via Abbondanza, Pompeii's main street. Lined with shops, bars, and restaurants, it was a lively, pedestrian-only zone. The three "beaver-teeth" stones are traffic barriers that kept chariots out. On the corner (just to the left), take a close look at the dark travertine column standing next to the white one. Notice that the marble drums of the white column are not chiseled entirely round—another construction project left unfinished when Vesuvius erupted.

• *Head toward Vesuvius, walking along the right side of the Forum. Immediately to the right of the Temple of Jupiter, a door leads into the market hall, where you'll find two glass cases.*

❻ Fish and Produce Market— Plaster Casts of Victims

As the frescoes on the wall (just inside on the left) indicate, this is where Pompeiians came to buy their food—fish, bread, chickens, and so on. These fine examples of Roman art—with their glimpses of everyday life and mastery of depth and illusion—would not be matched until the Renaissance, a thousand years after the fall of Rome.

The glass cases hold casts of Pompeiians, eerily captured in their last moments. They were quickly suffocated by a superheated avalanche of gas and ash, and their bodies were encased in volcanic debris. While excavating, modern archaeologists detected hollow spaces underfoot, created when the victims' bodies decomposed. By gently filling the holes with plaster, the archaeologists were able to create molds of the Pompeiians who were caught in the disaster.

• *Continue on, leaving the Forum through an arch behind the Temple of Jupiter. Here you'll find a pedestrian-only road sign (ahead on the right corner, above the* REG VII INS IV *sign) and more "beaver-teeth" traffic blocks. The modern cafeteria is the only eatery inside the archaeological site (with a coffee bar and WC). Twenty yards past the cafeteria, on the left-hand side at #24, is the entrance to the...*

❼ Baths of the Forum (Terme del Foro)

Pompeii had six public baths, each with a men's and a women's section. You're in the men's zone. The leafy courtyard at the entrance was the gymnasium. After working out, clients could relax with a hot bath *(caldarium)*, warm bath *(tepidarium)*, or cold plunge *(frigidarium)*.

The first big, plain room you enter served as the **dressing room**. Holes on the walls were for pegs to hang clothing. The window (with Neptune underneath) was originally covered with a less-translucent Roman glass. Walk over the non-slip mosaics into the next room.

The *tepidarium* is ringed by mini-statues or *telamones* (male caryatids, figures used as supporting pillars), which divided the lockers. Clients would undress and warm up here, perhaps stretching out on one of the bronze benches near the bronze heater for a massage. Look at the ceiling—half crushed by the eruption and half intact, with its fine blue-and-white stucco work.

Next, admire the engineering in the steam-bath room, or *caldarium*. The double floor was heated from below—so nice with bare feet (look into the grate to see the brick support towers). The double walls with brown terra-cotta tiles held the heat. Romans soaked in the big tub, which was filled with hot water. Opposite the big tub is a fountain, which spouted water onto the hot floor, creating steam. The lettering on the fountain reminded those enjoying the room which two politicians paid for it...and how much it cost them (5,250 *sestertii*). To keep condensation from dripping annoyingly from the ceiling, fluting (ribbing) was added to carry water down the walls.

• *Today's visitors exit the baths through the original entry. If you're a bit hungry, immediately across the street is an ancient...*

❽ Fast-Food Joint

After a bath, it was only natural to want a little snack. So, just across the street is a fast-food joint, marked by a series of rectangular marble counters. Most ancient Romans didn't cook for themselves in their tiny apartments, so to-go places like this were commonplace. The holes in the counters held the pots for food. Each container was like a thermos, with a wooden lid to keep the soup hot, the wine cool, and so on. Notice the groove in the front doorstep and the holes out on the curb. The holes likely accommodated cords for stretching awnings over the sidewalk to shield the clientele from the hot sun, while the grooves were for the shop's folding accordion doors. Look at the wheel grooves in the pavement, worn down through centuries of use. There are also more stepping-stones for pedestrians to cross the flooded streets.

• *Just a few steps uphill from the fast-food joint is the...*

❾ House of the Tragic Poet (Casa de Poeta Tragico)

This house is typical Roman style. The entry is flanked by two family-owned shops (each with a track for a collapsing accordion door). The home is like a train running straight away from the street: atrium (with skylight and pool to catch the rain), den (where deals were made by the shopkeeper), and garden (with rooms facing it and a shrine to remember both the gods and family ancestors). In the entryway is the famous "Beware of Dog" *(Cave Canem)* mosaic.

Today's visitors enter the home by the back door (circle around to the left). The modern pipe exposed across the lane is the same as ones used in the ancient plumbing system, hidden beneath the raised sidewalk. Inside the house, the grooves on the marble well-head were formed by generations of inhabitants dragging the bucket up by rope. The richly frescoed dining room is off the garden. Diners lounged on their couches (the Roman custom) and enjoyed frescoes with fake "windows," giving the illusion of a bigger and airier room. Just to the right is a humble BBQ-style kitchen with a little closet for the toilet (the kitchen and bathroom shared the same plumbing).

• *Return to the fast-food place and continue about 10 yards downhill to the big intersection. From the center of the intersection, look left to see a giant arch, framing a nice view of Mount Vesuvius.*

❿ Aqueduct Arch—Running Water

Water was critical for this city of 20,000 people, and this arch was part of Pompeii's water-delivery system. A 100-mile-long aqueduct carried fresh water down from the hillsides to a big reservoir perched at the highest point of the city wall. Since overall water pressure was disappointing, Pompeians built arches like the brick one you see here (originally covered in marble) with hidden water tanks at the top. Located just below the altitude of the main tank, these smaller tanks were filled by gravity, and provided each neighborhood with reliable pressure.

• *If you're thirsty, fill your water bottle from the modern fountain. Then continue straight downhill one block (50 yards) to #2 on the left.*

⓫ House of the Faun (Casa del Founo)

Stand across the street and marvel at the grand entry with *"HAVE"* (hail to you) as a welcome mat. Go in. Notice the two shrines above the entryway—one dedicated to the gods, the other to this wealthy family's ancestors.

You are standing in Pompeii's largest home, where you're greeted by the delightful small bronze statue of the *Dancing Faun,* famed for its realistic movement and fine proportion. (The origi-

nal is in Naples' Archaeological Museum.)
With 40 rooms and 27,000 square feet,
the House of the Faun covers an entire
city block. The next floor mosaic, with
an intricate diamond-like design, deco-
rates the homeowner's office. Beyond that
is the famous floor mosaic of the *Battle
of Alexander*. (The original is also at the
museum in Naples.) In 333 B.C., Alexander
the Great beat Darius and the Persians.
Romans had great respect for Alexander,
the first great emperor before Rome's.
While most of Pompeii's nouveau riche
had notoriously bad taste and stuffed their

NAPLES

palaces with over-the-top, mismatched decor, this guy had class.
Both the faun (an ancient copy of a famous Greek statue) and the
Alexander mosaic show an appreciation for history.

The house's back courtyard leads to the exit in the far-right
corner. It's lined with pillars rebuilt after the A.D. 62 earthquake.
Take a close look at the brick, mortar, and fake marble stucco
veneer.

• *Sneak out of the House of the Faun through its back door and turn
right. (If this exit is closed, return to the entrance and make a U-turn
left, around to the back of the house.) Thirty yards down, along the right-
hand side of the street are metal cages protecting...*

⓬ Original Lead Pipes

These 2,000-year-old pipes (made of lead imported from Britannia)
were part of the city's elaborate water system. From the aqueduct-
fed water tank at the high end of town, three independent pipe
systems supplied water to the city: one for baths, one for private
homes, and one for public water fountains. If there was a water
shortage, democratic priorities prevailed: First the baths were cut
off, then the private homes. The last water supply to go was the
public fountains, where all citizens could get drinking and cooking
water.

• *If the street's not closed off, take your first left (on Vicolo dei Vettii),
walk about 20 yards, and find the entrance (on the left) to the...*

⓭ House of the Vettii (Casa dei Vettii)

Pompeii's best-preserved home has been completely blocked off for
years; unfortunately it's unlikely to reopen in time for your visit.
The House of the Vettii was the bachelor pad of two wealthy merchant brothers. If you can see the entryway, you may spot the huge
erection. This is not pornography. There's a meaning here: The penis
and the sack of money balance each other on the goldsmith scale

above a fine bowl of fruit. Translation: Only with a balance of fertility and money can you have abundance.

If it's open, step into the atrium with its ceiling open to the sky to collect light and rainwater. The pool, while decorative, was a functional water-supply tank. It's flanked by large money boxes anchored to the floor. The brothers were certainly successful merchants, and possibly moneylenders, too.

Exit on the right, passing the tight servant quarters, and go into the kitchen, with its bronze cooking pots (and an exposed lead pipe on the back wall). The passage dead-ends in the little Venus Room, which features erotic frescoes behind glass.

Return to the atrium and pass into the big colonnaded garden. It was replanted according to the plan indicated by the traces of roots that were excavated from the volcanic ash. Richly frescoed entertainment rooms ring this courtyard. Circle counterclockwise. The dining room is finely decorated in black and "Pompeiian red" (from iron rust). Study the detail. Notice the lead humidity seal between the wall and the floor, designed to keep the moisture-sensitive frescoes dry. (Had Leonardo da Vinci taken this clever step, his *Last Supper* in Milan might be in better shape today.) Continuing around, you'll see more of the square white stones inlaid in the floor. Imagine them reflecting like cats' eyes as the brothers and their friends wandered around by oil lamp late at night. Frescoes in the Yellow Room (near the exit) show off the ancient mastery of perspective, which would not be matched elsewhere in Europe for nearly 1,500 years.

• *Facing the entrance to the House of the Vettii, turn left and walk downhill one long block (along Vicolo dei Vettii) to a T-intersection (Via della Fortuna), marked by a stone fountain with a bull's head for a spout. Intersections like this were busy neighborhood centers, where the rent was highest and people gathered. With the fountain at your back, turn left, then immediately right, walking along a gently curving road (Vicolo Storto). On the left side of the street, at #22, find four big stone cylinders.*

NAPLES

ⓔ Bakery and Mill (Forno e Mulini)

The brick oven looks like a modern-day pizza oven. The stubby stone towers are flour grinders. Grain was poured into the top, and

donkeys or slaves pushed wooden bars that turned the stones. The powdered grain dropped out of the bottom as flour—flavored with tiny bits of rock. Each neighborhood had a bakery like this.

Continue to the next intersection (Via degli Augustali, where there's another fast-food joint) and turn left. As you walk, look

at the destructive power of all the vines, and notice how deeply the chariot grooves have worn into the pavement. Deep grooves could break wagon wheels. The suddenly ungroovy stretch indicates that this road was in the process of being repaved when the eruption shut everything down.

• *Head about 50 yards down this (obviously one-way) street to #44 (on the left). Here you'll find the Taberna Hedones (with a small atrium, den, and garden). This bar still has its original floor and, deeper in, the mosaic arch of a grotto fountain. Just past the tavern, turn right and walk downhill to #18, on the right.*

ⓞ Brothel (Lupanare)

You'll find the biggest crowds in Pompeii at a place that was likely popular 2,000 ago, too—the brothel. Prostitutes were nicknamed *lupe* (she-wolves), alluding to the call they made when trying to attract business. The brothel was a simple place, with beds and pillows made of stone. The ancient graffiti includes tallies and exotic names of the women, indicating the prostitutes came from all corners of the Mediterranean (it also served as feedback from satisfied customers). The faded frescoes above the cells may have been a kind of menu for services offered. Note the idealized women (white, which was considered beautiful; one wears an early bra) and the rougher men (dark, considered horny). The bed legs came with little disk-like barriers to keep critters from crawling up.

• *Leaving the brothel, go right, then take the first left, and continue going downhill two blocks to the intersection with Pompeii's main drag, Via dell'Abbondanza. The Forum—and exit—are to the right, for those who may wish to opt out from here.*

The huge amphitheater—which is certainly skippable—is 10 minutes to your left. But for now, go left for 60 yards, then turn right just beyond the fountain, and walk down Via dei Teatri. Turn left before the columns (about 50 yards away), and head downhill another 60 yards to #28, which marks the...

NAPLES

⓰ Temple of Isis

This Egyptian temple served Pompeii's Egyptian community. The little white stucco shrine with the plastic roof housed holy water from the Nile. Isis, from Egyptian myth, was one of many foreign gods adopted by the eclectic Romans. Pompeii must have had a synagogue, too, but it has yet to be excavated.

• *Exit the temple where you entered, and go right. At the next intersection, turn right again, and head downhill to the adjacent theaters. Your goal is the large theater down the corridor at #20, but if it's closed, look at the smaller but similar theater (Teatro Piccolo) just beyond at #19.*

⓱ Theater

Originally a Greek theater (Greeks built theirs with the help of a hillside), this was the birthplace of the Greek port here in 470

b.c. During Roman times, the theater sat 5,000 people in three sets of seats, all with different prices: the five marble terraces up close (filled with romantic wooden seats for two), the main section, and the cheap nosebleed section (surviving only on the right). The square stones above the cheap seats once supported a canvas rooftop. Take note of the high-profile boxes, flanking the stage, for guests of honor. From this perch, you can see the gladiator barracks—the colonnaded courtyard beyond the theater. They lived in tiny rooms, trained in the courtyard, and fought in the nearby amphitheater.

• *You've seen Pompeii's highlights. When you're ready to leave, backtrack to the main road and turn left, going uphill to the Forum, where you'll find the main entrance/exit.*

   However, there's much more to see—three-quarters of Pompeii's 164 acres have been excavated, but this tour has covered only a third of the site. After the theater—if you still have energy to see more—go back to the main road, and take a right toward the eastern part of the site, where the crowds thin out. Go straight for about 10 minutes, then turn right down a dirt path (about 75 yards from the wall at the edge of the site), which leads to the...

⓲ Amphitheater

Climb to the upper level of the amphitheater (if the external stairs are blocked, try the entrance to the left). With Vesuvius looming in the background, mentally replace the tourists below with gladiators and wild animals locked in combat. Walk along the top of the amphitheater and look down into the grassy rectangular area surrounded by columns. This is the **Palaestra,** an area once used for athletic training. Facing the other way, look for the bell tower that tops the roofline of the modern city of Pompei, where locals go about their daily lives in the shadow of the volcano, just as their ancestors did 2,000 years ago. *HAVE!*

Herculaneum (Ercolano)

Smaller, less crowded, and not as ruined as its famous big sister, Herculaneum (worth ▲▲) offers a closer, more intimate peek into ancient Roman life but lacks the grandeur of Pompeii (there's barely a colonnade).

Cost and Hours: €11, €20 combo-ticket includes Pompeii and three lesser sites (valid 3 consecutive days). Open daily April-Oct 8:30-19:30, Nov-March 8:30-17:00, ticket office closes 1.5 hours earlier (tel. 081-777-7008, www.pompeiisites .org).

Getting There: Herculaneum (Ercolano) is about 25 minutes from Naples and roughly 45 minutes from Sorrento on the same Circumvesuviana train that goes to Pompeii. Get off at the Ercolano Scavi train stop. To walk to the ruins, leave the Ercolano station and turn right, then left; go eight blocks straight downhill from the station to the end of the road, where you'll see the entrance marked by a grand arch. (Skip Museo MAV.) Pass through the arch and continue down the path, taking in the bird's-eye first impression of the site. The ticket office, baggage storage (pick up bags 30 minutes prior to site closing), and WCs are located in the modern building, 200 yards ahead.

Information: Pick up a free detailed map and excellent booklet (with numbered explanations of each building) at the info desk next to the ticket window. The site also has a bookstore.

Audioguide: The informative and interesting audioguide sheds light on the ruins and life in Herculaneum in the first century A.D. (€6.50, €10/2 people, ID required, pick up 100 yards after the ticket turnstiles).

Length of This Tour: Allow one hour.

❯ **Self-Guided Tour:** Caked and baked by the same A.D. 79 eruption that pummeled Pompeii, Herculaneum is a small community of intact buildings with plenty of surviving detail. While

Pompeii was initially smothered in ash, Herculaneum was spared at first—due to the direction of the wind—but got slammed about 12 hours after the eruption started by a superheated avalanche of ash and hot gases roaring off the volcano. The city was eventually buried under nearly 60 feet of superheated ash, which hardened into tuff, perfectly preserving the city until excavations began in 1748.

After leaving the ticket window, walk the long path around the site to the entrance. From here, you can get a sense of just how much volcanic material piled up. The present-day city of Ercolano looms just above, and the modern buildings don't look much different from their ancient counterparts.

After crossing the modern bridge into the excavation site, stroll straight to the end of the street and find the **Seat of the Augustali** (Sede degli Augustali). Decorated with frescoes of Hercules (for whom this city was named), it was a forum for freed slaves climbing their way up the ladder of Roman society.

Leave the building through the back and go to the right, down the lane. The adjacent *thermopolium* (at #19) was the Roman equivalent to a fast food joint, with giant jars for wine, oil, and snacks. Most of the buildings along here were shops, with apartments above. Look around doorways for ancient bits of wood charred by the pyroclastic flows. Most buildings were made of stone, but the floors and beams were wood (which doesn't survive at any other ancient site).

A few steps on, at #14, the **Bottega ad Cucumas** wine shop still has charred remains of beams, and its drink list remains frescoed on the outside wall.

Take the next right, go halfway down, and on the left find the **House of Neptune and Amphitrite** (Casa di Nettuno e Anfitrite). Outside, notice the intact upper floor and imagine it going even higher. Inside, you'll see colorful mosaics and a unique "frame" made of shells.

Back outside, continue downhill to the intersection, then head left to the far end of the site and the don't-miss-it **gymnasium** *(palestra)* complex. The highlight is the Hydra of Lerna, a sculpted bronze fountain that features the seven-headed monster defeated by Hercules as one of his 12 labors. Find the Hydra by walking through the triangular-shaped entrances carved in the tuff wall. To light up this cavernous space, go to the second doorway on the left wall and press the switch. Just outside, take a close look at the "marble" columns, which are actually made of rounded bricks covered with a thick layer of plaster, shaped to look like carved marble. While important buildings in Rome had solid marble columns, these are typical of ordinary buildings.

Downhill at #21, the **House of the Deer** (Casa dei Cervi) is also worth seeking out. It's named for the statues of deer being attacked by dogs in the garden courtyard (these are copies; the originals are in the Archaeological Museum in Naples). As you wander through the rooms, notice the colorfully frescoed walls. Ancient Herculaneum, like all Roman cities of that age, was filled with color, rather than the stark white we often imagine (even the statues were painted).

Continuing downhill, the **baths** (Terme Suburbane, enter near the side of the statue, sometimes closed) illustrate the city's devastation. After you descend into the baths, look back at the steps. You'll see the original wood charred in the disaster, protected by the wooden planks you just walked on. At the bottom of the stairs, in the waiting room to the right, notice where the floor collapsed under the sheer weight of the volcanic debris. (The sunken pavement reveals the baths' heating system: hot air generated by wood-burning furnaces and circulated between the different levels of the floor.) A doorway in front of the stairs is still filled with solidified ash. Despite the damage, elements of refinement remain intact, such as the delicate stuccoes in the *caldarium* (hot bath).

Back outside, make your way down the steps to the sunken area just below. As you descend, you're walking across what was formerly Herculaneum's beach (the shoreline was extended outward by material from the volcano). Looking back, you'll see **arches** that were part of boat storage areas. Archaeologists used to wonder why so few victims were found in Herculaneum. But during excavations in 1981, hundreds of skeletons were discovered here, between the wall of volcanic stone behind you and the city in front of you. Some of Herculaneum's 4,000 citizens tried to escape by sea, but were overtaken by the pyroclastic flows.

Thankfully, your escape is easier. Either follow the sounds of the water and continue through the tunnel; or, more scenically, backtrack and exit the same way you entered.

Vesuvius

The 4,000-foot-high Vesuvius, mainland Europe's only active volcano, has been sleeping restlessly since 1944. Up here, it's desolate and lunar-like, and the rocks are newly created. Walk the entire accessible part of the crater lip for the most interesting views; the far end overlooks Pompeii. Be still. Listen to the wind and the occasional cascades of rocks tumbling into the crater. Any steam? Vesuvius is closed to visitors when erupting.

Cost and Hours: €8, which includes a mandatory guide who provides a brief introduction, then sets you free (daily April-Oct 9:00-17:00, until 18:00 in summer, Nov-March 9:00-15:00, no WC, tel. 081-865-3911, www.parco nazionaledelvesuvio.it).

Getting to Vesuvius: The summit is accessible year-round by car (just drive to the end of the road and pay €2.50 to park), by taxi (€90 round-trip from Naples including a 2-hour wait, cheaper from Pompeii), or by bus. From the parking lot, it's a

steep 30-minute hike to the top for a sweeping view of the Bay of Naples. Bring a coat; it's often cold and windy (especially Oct-April).

From **Pompeii,** you have two bus services to choose from, each taking about three hours (including 1.25 hours at the top). The UnicoCampania bus—marked *EAVBUS* or *City Sightseeing Napoli*—goes up the main road and lets you return on any scheduled departure (€10 round-trip plus €8 summit admission, 12/day, weather permitting in winter, departs from Piazza Anfiteatro, Piazza Esedra in front of TI, and Pompei Scavi Circumvesuviana station, tel. 081-551-3109, www.unicocampania.it).

Busvia del Vesuvio winds you up a bumpy private road through the back of the national park in a cross between a shuttle bus and a monster truck. It's a fun, more scenic way to go, but not for the easily queasy (€19 includes summit admission, runs hourly April-Oct daily 9:00-15:00, also at 16:00 June-Aug, Nov-March runs rarely—call for schedule, departs from Camping Zeus near Pompei Scavi Circumvesuviana station, tel. 081-861-5320, www.busviadelvesuvio.com).

From **Herculaneum,** your best bet is the Vesuvio Express, which makes the trip in small vans from Herculaneum's Ercolano Scavi Circumvesuviana station (€10 round-trip plus €8 summit admission, daily from 9:00, runs every 45 minutes based on demand, about 2.5 hours, tel. 081-739-3666, www.vesuvio express.it).

SORRENTO AND CAPRI

Without a hint of big-city Naples and just an hour to the south, serene Sorrento makes an ideal home base for exploring all the fascinating sights in the region, from Naples to the Amalfi Coast to Paestum. And the jetsetting island of Capri is just a short cruise from Sorrento, offering more charm and fun (outside of the crowded months of July and August) than its glitzy reputation would lead you to believe.

Sorrento

Wedged on a ledge under the mountains and over the Mediterranean, spritzed by lemon and olive groves, Sorrento is an attractive resort of 20,000 residents and, in summer, just as many tourists. It's as well-located for regional sightseeing as it is a fine place to stay and stroll. The Sorrentines have gone out of their way to create a completely safe and relaxed place for tourists to come and spend money. Everyone seems to speak fluent English and work for the Chamber of Commerce. This gateway to the Amalfi Coast has an unspoiled old quarter, a lively main shopping street, and a spectacular cliffside setting. Residents are proud of the many world-class romantics who've vacationed here, such as the famed tenor Enrico Caruso, who chose Sorrento as the place to spend his last weeks in 1921.

SORRENTO AND CAPRI

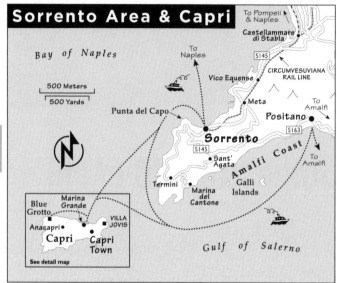

Planning Your Time

With Sorrento as your home base, spend a minimum of three days and nights in the region. On your way to or from Sorrento, visit Naples as a day trip. After settling in Sorrento, spend a day touring the Amalfi Coast by bus, and another day split between Sorrento and Pompeii (accessible by Circumvesuviana train). With more time, catch a quick boat ride to the nearby island of Capri or linger on the Amalfi Coast (see next chapter), heading as far south as Paestum's Greek temples.

Orientation to Sorrento

Sorrento is long and narrow. The main drag, Corso Italia (50 yards in front of the Circumvesuviana train station), runs parallel

to the sea from the station through the town center and out to the cape, where the road's name becomes Via Capo. Piazza Tasso marks the town's center. Everything mentioned here (except the hotels on Via Capo) is within a 10-minute walk of the train station. Sorrento hibernates in January and February, when many places close down.

Tourist Information

The TI (labeled *Soggiorno e Turismo*)—located inside the Foreigners' Club—hands out the free monthly *Surrentum* magazine, with a great city map and schedules of boats, buses, concerts, and festivals (Mon-Fri 8:30-16:15, closed Sat-Sun, Via Luigi de Maio 35, tel. 081-807-4033, www.sorrentotourism.com). If you arrive after the TI closes, look for their useful handouts in the lobby of the Foreigners' Club (open until midnight).

To get from the train station to the TI, head straight out to Corso Italia and turn left. Walk five minutes to Piazza Tasso, turn right at the end of the square, and go down Via Luigi de Maio through Piazza Sant'Antonino, bearing right downhill about 30 yards to the Foreigners' Club mansion at #35.

If you just need quick advice, the fake tourist office—located in a green caboose just outside the train station—can be of help. While they're a private business with hopes that you'll purchase one of their overpriced excursions, they're willing to give basic information on directions, buses, and ferries.

Arrival in Sorrento

By Train: Those arriving by train (Sorrento is the last stop on the Circumvesuviana train line) will see the Amalfi bus stop, as well as taxis waiting to overcharge them. All recommended hotels—except those on Via Capo—are within a 10-minute walk (a much cheaper mode of transport than the €15 fare taxi drivers will gouge you).

By Boat: Passenger boats dock at Marina Piccola, Sorrento's little harbor. To get to Piazza Tasso, it's a 15-minute uphill hike or a short ride on a small blue bus (4/hour, €1, buy ticket from driver, day passes not valid) or a red-and-white bus (3/hour, buy €1 tickets at the tobacco shop or adjacent kiosk).

Helpful Hints

Church Services: The **cathedral** hosts an English-language Anglican service at 17:00 most Sundays mid-April-July and Sept-Oct. At **Santa Maria delle Grazie** (perhaps the most beautiful Baroque church in town), cloistered nuns sing from above and out of sight during a Mass each morning at 7:30 (on Via delle Grazie).

Bookstore: Libreria Tasso has a decent selection of books in English, including this one (Mon-Sat 10:00-13:20 & 16:30-21:30, Sun 11:30-13:15 & 19:00-22:00, shorter hours off-season; Via San Cesareo 96, one block north of cathedral, near Sorrento Men's Club; tel. 081-807-1639).

Laundry: Sorrento has two handy launderettes. One is at Corso

Italia 30 (daily May-Sept 7:00-24:00, Oct-April 8:00-23:00; full-service—€12/load, drop off: 8:00-13:00 & 16:00-19:30, drop before 9:30 for same-day turnaround; self-service—€6/ load wash and dry, includes soap; for self-service, enter through alley; tel. 081-878-1185). The other launderette is at the corner of Corso Italia and Via degli Aranci (daily 8:00-22:00, self-service-€8/load, includes soap).

Travel Agency: Top Level Travel books train tickets, flights, and more (Mon-Sat 9:00-13:00 & 16:00-20:00, closed Sun, Via degli Aranci 67, tel. 081-877-4742). Exiting the train station, go left around the station and go up the stairs—it's on the first floor next to Bar Paradise.

Local Guides: Giovanna Donadio is a good tour guide for Sorrento, Amalfi, and Capri (€100/half-day, €160/day, same price for any size of group, mobile 338-466-0114, giovanna _dona@hotmail.com). **Giovanni Visetti** is a nature-lover who organizes hikes (www.giovistravels.com).

Where It's At: The **Foreigners' Club** provides reasonably priced snacks and drinks, music, dancing, and magnificent vistas from its cliffside terrace—drop in for the view overlooking the harbor and the Bay of Naples (daily 9:30-24:00, behind TI, public WC, Via Luigi de Maio 35, tel. 081-877-3263). Also see "Nightlife in Sorrento" and "Eating in Sorrento," later in this chapter.

Getting Around Sorrento

By Bus: City buses (either orange or red-and-white) all stop near the main square, Piazza Tasso. Bus #A runs to Meta beach or the hotels on Via Capo, buses #B and #C go to the port (Marina Piccola), and bus #D heads to the fishing village (Marina Grande). Buses #A and #D stop at the beginning of Corso Italia (west side of Piazza Tasso for Via Capo or Marina Grande, east side for Meta); #B and #C stop at the corner of Piazza Sant'Antonino, just down the hill towards the water. Tickets for a ride between just the port and Piazza Tasso cost €1 (see "Arrival in Sorrento," earlier); other tickets cost €2.40 and are good for 45 minutes (purchase at tobacco shops and newsstands). Stamp your ticket upon entering the bus. The one-day pass (€7.20) and three-day pass (€18) are also valid for the entire Amalfi Coast.

By Rental Wheels: Many places rent motor scooters for about €35 per day, including **Europcar** (Mon-Sat 9:00-13:00 & 16:00-19:30, closed Sun, Corso Italia 210p, tel. 081-878-4956, www.sorrento.it) and **Penisola Rent,** a half-block away (daily 9:00-13:00 & 16:00-20:30, located in Hotel Nice, tel. 081-877-4664, www.penisolarent.com). Don't rent a car in summer unless you enjoy traffic jams.

By Taxi: Taxis are expensive, charging at least €15 for the short ride from the station to hotels. Because of heavy traffic and the complex one-way road system, you can often walk faster than you can ride. If you do use a taxi, even if you agree to a set price, be sure it has a meter (all official taxis have one). I think taxis are a huge rip-off, since city officials don't have the nerve to regulate them, and hotels are afraid to alienate them. Take the bus instead.

Self-Guided Walk

Welcome to Sorrento

Get to know Sorrento with this lazy self-guided town stroll.

• *Begin on the main square. Stand under the flags with your back to the sea, and face...*

Piazza Tasso: As in any southern Italian town, this "piazza" is Sorrento's living room. It may be noisy and congested, but locals want to be where the action is...and be part of the scene. The most expensive apartments and top cafés are on or near this square. Buses stop near here on their way to Marina Piccola (where boats depart from the harbor for Naples and Capri, a 10-minute hike below you), to the train station (left), and to Via Capo (right).

This square spans a gorge that divided the town until the 19th century. The old town (on your right) still has some surviving ancient Greek streets. The new town (to your left) was farm country just two centuries ago. A statue of St. Anthony, patron of Sorrento, faces north as if greeting those coming from Naples (often equipped with an armload of fresh lemons and oranges). If you walk a block inland, go right up to the green railing, and look down, you'll see steps that were carved in the fifth century B.C.

Sorrento's name came from the Greek word for "siren," the legendary half-bird, half-woman who sang an intoxicating lullaby. According to Homer, the sirens lived on an island near here. No one had ever sailed by the sirens without succumbing to their incredible musical charms...and to death. But Homer's hero Ulysses was determined to hear the song. He put wax in his oarsmen's ears and had himself lashed to the mast of his ship. Oh, it was nice. The sirens, thinking they had lost their powers, threw themselves into the sea, and the place became safe to inhabit. Ulysses' odyssey was all about the westward expansion of Greek culture, and to the ancient Greeks, places like Sorrento were the wild, wild west.

• *With your back still to the sea, head to the far-right corner of the square, behind the statue of Torquato Tasso, the square's namesake. (A Sorrento native, he was a lively Renaissance poet.) Peek into the big courtyard of Palazzo Correale (#18, behind the statue in the right corner) to get a feel for an 18th-century aristocratic palace's courtyard, lined*

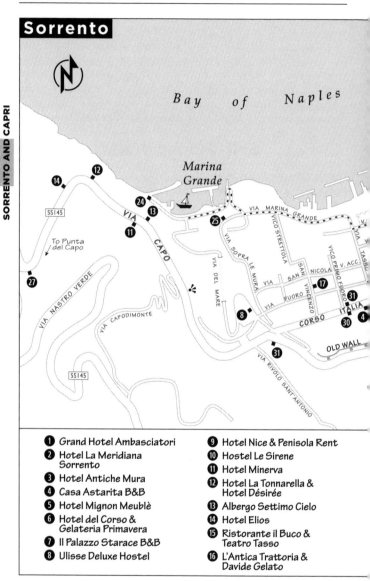

Sorrento

SORRENTO AND CAPRI

① Grand Hotel Ambasciatori
② Hotel La Meridiana Sorrento
③ Hotel Antiche Mura
④ Casa Astarita B&B
⑤ Hotel Mignon Meublè
⑥ Hotel del Corso & Gelateria Primavera
⑦ Il Palazzo Starace B&B
⑧ Ulisse Deluxe Hostel
⑨ Hotel Nice & Penisola Rent
⑩ Hostel Le Sirene
⑪ Hotel Minerva
⑫ Hotel La Tonnarella & Hotel Désirée
⑬ Albergo Settimo Cielo
⑭ Hotel Elios
⑮ Ristorante il Buco & Teatro Tasso
⑯ L'Antica Trattoria & Davide Gelato

with characteristic tiles. Next door, a fun shop sells regional products and offers free biscuits and tastes of liqueurs. As you're leaving the court-yard, on your immediate left you'll see the narrow...

Via Santa Maria della Pietà: Here, just a few yards off the noisy main drag, is a street that goes back centuries before Christ. About 100 yards down the lane, at #24, find a 13th-century palace (no balconies back then...for security reasons), now an elementary

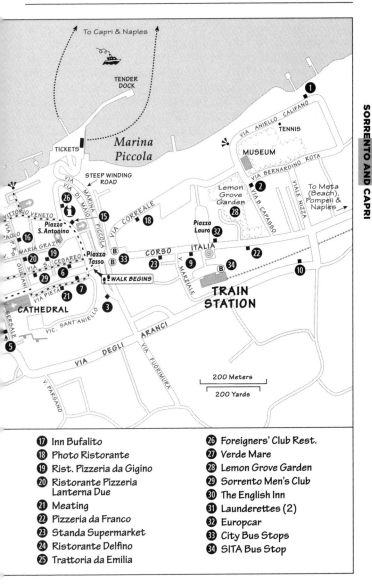

17 Inn Bufalito
18 Photo Ristorante
19 Rist. Pizzeria da Gigino
20 Ristorante Pizzeria Lanterna Due
21 Meating
22 Pizzeria da Franco
23 Standa Supermarket
24 Ristorante Delfino
25 Trattoria da Emilia

26 Foreigners' Club Rest.
27 Verde Mare
28 Lemon Grove Garden
29 Sorrento Men's Club
30 The English Inn
31 Launderettes (2)
32 Europcar
33 City Bus Stops
34 SITA Bus Stop

school. A few steps farther on, you'll see a tiny shrine across the street. Typical of southern Italy, it's where the faithful pray to their saint, who contacts Mary, who contacts Jesus, who contacts God. This shrine is a bit more direct—it starts right with Mary.

• Continue down the lane, which ends at the...

Cathedral: This is the seat of the local bishop. Pop in for a cool stroll around the ambulatory, checking out the impressive *intarsio* (inlaid-wood) doors. Two sets, inlaid on both sides, show many scenes of the town and its industry. The doors facing the main street include an old town map. These were made to celebrate the pope's visit in 1992. Also notice the intricate inlaid Stations of the Cross, which describe Jesus' last hours.

• *Backtrack 10 yards down Via Santa Maria della Pietà, turn left, cross busy Corso Italia (look back at the bell tower, with its ancient Roman columns at the base), and go straight on Via P. Reginaldo Giuliani, following the...*

Old Greek Street Plan: Notice here how streets are laid out—east-west for the most sunlight and north-south for the prevailing and cooling breeze.

• *One block ahead is a fine old portico, the...*

Sorrento Men's Club: Once the meeting place of the town's nobles, this club has been a retreat for retired working-class men for generations. Strictly no women—and no phones.

Italian men venerate their mothers. (Italians joke that Jesus must have been a southern Italian because his mother believed her son was God, he believed his mom was a virgin, and he lived at home with her until he was 30.) But Italian men have also built into their culture ways to be on their own. Here, men play cards and gossip under a historic emblem of the city and a finely frescoed 16th-century dome, with its marvelous 3-D scenes.

• *At the Men's Club, turn right onto...*

Via San Cesareo: This touristy pedestrian-only shopping street leads four or five blocks back to Piazza Tasso. All along the way, you can peruse (and sample) lemon products in the very competitive shops. Notice the huge ancient doorways with their tiny doors—to let the right people in, carefully, during a more-dangerous age.

• *At the noisy street on the edge of Piazza Tasso, turn left and fight the traffic downhill to the next square, with another...*

Statue of St. Anthony (Antonino): Sorrento's town saint humbly looms among the palms, facing the basilica where his reliquary lies (under the altar in the crypt, surrounded by lots of votives). From here, you can quit the walk and stay in the city center, or continue to the village-like waterfront (if it's before 20:00, you can catch a bus to get back).

• *Exit the square diagonally to the left and gradually wind your way downhill toward Marina Grande (not down the street that leads to the Foreigners' Club and port). After a block or so, on the right you'll see the trees in front of the Imperial Hotel Tramontano, and to their right a path leading to a...*

Cliffside Square: This fine public square, the Villa Comunale, overlooks the harbor. Belly up to the banister to enjoy the view of the little harbor and the Bay of Naples. From here, steps zigzag down to Marina Piccola, where lounge chairs, filled by vacationers working on tans, line the sundecks. The Franciscan church fronting this square has a great little cloister (pop in to see Sicilian Gothic—a 13th-century mix of Norman, Gothic, and Arabic styles).

• *Return to the road and continue downhill, walking through the next square (Piazza della Vittoria), which offers another grand view. Stay on the road closest to the water—it eventually leads to stairs that zigzag down to Marina Grande, Sorrento's big harbor. Just before reaching the harbor, you pass under an...*

Ancient Greek Gate: This gate is a reminder that Marina Grande is a separate town from Sorrento, with its own proud residents. It's said that even their cats look different. Because Marina Grande dwellers lived outside the wall and were more susceptible to rape, pillage, and plunder, Sorrentines believe that they come from Saracen (Turkish pirate) stock. Sorrentines still scare their children by saying, "Behave—or the Turks will take you away."

Marina Grande's economy is still based on its fishing fleet. People respect old traditions. Women wear black when a relative dies (one year for an uncle, aunt, or sibling; 2-3 years for a husband or parent). Men get off easy, just wearing a black button if their loved one dies.

There are two recommended restaurants on the harbor. **Trattoria da Emilia** has an old newspaper clipping, tacked near the door, about Sophia Loren filming here. On the far side of the harbor, **Ristorante Delfino** boasts a sundeck for a lazy drink before or after lunch.

From here, buses return to the center at Piazza Tasso every hour (€2.40, buy ticket at tobacco shop).

Sights in Sorrento

▲▲**Strolling**—Take time to explore the surprisingly pleasant old

city between Corso Italia and the sea. Views from the public park next to Imperial Hotel Tramontano are worth the detour. Each night in summer (May-Oct at 19:30; Nov-April weekends only), the police close off the Corso Italia to traffic, and Sorrento's main drag becomes a

Lemons

Around here, *limoni* are ubiquitous: screaming yellow painted on ceramics, dainty bottles of *limoncello,* and lemons the size of softballs at the fruit stand. The Amalfi Coast and Sorrento area produces several different kinds of lemons.

The gigantic bumpy lemons are actually citrons, called *cedri,* and are more for show—they're pulpier than they are juicy, and make a good marmalade. The juicy *sfusato sorrentino,* grown only in Sorrento, is shaped like an American football, while the *sfusato amalfitano,* with knobby points on both ends, is less juicy but equally aromatic. These two kinds of luscious lemons are used in sweets such as *granita* (shaved ice doused in lemonade), *limoncello* (a candy-like liqueur with a big kick, called *limoncino* on the Cinque Terre), *delizia* (a dome of fluffy cake filled and slathered with a thick whipped lemon cream), *spremuta di limone* (fresh-squeezed lemon juice), and, of course, gelato or *sorbetto alla limone.*

thriving people scene. The *passeggiata* peaks at about 22:00. (When Piazza Tasso and the main thoroughfare are closed to traffic, buses for Via Capo leave from up on Via degli Aranci, a short walk from Piazza Tasso along Via Fuorimura.)

Lemon Products Galore—Via San Cesareo is lined with hard-working rival shops selling a mind-boggling array of lemon products and offering samples of lots of sour goodies. Poke around for a pungent experience.

▲Lemon Grove Garden (Giardini di Cataldo)—This small park consists of an inviting organic lemon and orange grove lined with shady, welcoming paths. The owners of the grove are seasoned green thumbs, having worked the orchard through many generations. You'll see that they've even grafted orange-tree branches onto a lemon tree so that both fruits now grow on the same tree. The garden is dotted with benches, tables, and an inviting little tasting (and buying) stand. You'll get a chance to sniff and taste the varieties of lemons, and enjoy free samples of chilled *limoncello* along with various other homemade liqueurs made from basil, mandarins, or fennel (enthusiastically free, daily April-Sept 10:00-20:00, Oct-March 10:00-16:30, tel. 081-807-4040). The main shop selling their organic homemade products and tasty gelato is across from the Corso Italia entrance at #267; a smaller stand is inside.

Enter the garden either on Corso Italia (100 yards north of the train station—where painted tiles show lemon fantasies), or at the intersection of Via Capasso and Via Rota (next to the Hotel La Meridiana Sorrento).

▲**Swimming near Sorrento**—If you require immediate tanning, you can rent a chair on the pier by the port. There are no great beaches in Sorrento—the gravelly, jam-packed private beaches of **Marina Piccola** are more for partying than pampering, and there's just a tiny spot for public use.

A sandy beach is two miles away at **Meta.** While the Meta Circumvesuviana stop is a very long walk from the beach (or a €25 cab ride), the red-and-white bus #A goes directly from Piazza Tasso to the Meta beach (last stop, schedule posted for hourly returns). At Meta, you'll find pizzerias, snack bars, and a little free section of beach, but it's mostly dominated by several sprawling private-beach complexes—if you go, pay for a spot in one of these. Lido Metamare seems best (open May-Sept, €2.50 entry; lockable changing cabins, lounge chairs, and more available for an extra fee; tel. 081-532-2505). It's a very Italian scene—locals complain that it's "too local" (i.e., inundated with Naples' riffraff)—with light lunches, a playground, a manicured beach, loud pop music...and no international tourists.

Tarzan might take Jane to the wild and stony beach at **Punta del Capo,** a 15-minute bus ride from Piazza Tasso (2/hour, get off at stop in front of the American Bar, then walk 10 minutes past ruined Roman Villa di Pollio). From the American Bar bus stop, you can also walk to **Marina di Puolo,** a tiny fishing town popular in the summer for its sandy beach, surfside restaurants, and beachfront disco (15-minute walk, follow signs).

Tennis—The Sorrento Sport Snack Bar has two fine courts open to the public (daily 9:30-23:00, until 20:00 in winter, €12/hour including rackets and balls for two people, call for reservation, across from recommended Grand Hotel Ambasciatori at Via Califano 5, tel. 081-807-1616).

Scuba Diving—To escape the shops, dive deep into the Mediterranean. PADI-certified Futuro Mare offers a one-hour boat ride out to the protected marine zone that lies between Sorrento and Capri, where you can try the beginners' dive (€90, includes instruction and complete supervision, April-Oct usually daily at 9:30). The boat also takes experienced certified divers (1 dive-€60, 2 dives-€95, April-Oct daily at 9:30 and 14:00). The whole experience takes about three hours. Prices include all equipment, transportation, and the dive itself, which lasts about 40 minutes for both novices and experts (call a day or two in advance to reserve, tel. 081-877-1472, mobile 349-653-6323, www.sorrento diving.it).

Boat Rental—You can rent motor boats big enough for four people (€150/day, plus gas—figure about €30 for a trip to Capri, more with a skipper; with your back to the ferry-ticket offices, it's to the left around the corner at Via Marina Piccola 43; tel. 081-807-2283, www.nauticasicsic.com).

Nightlife in Sorrento

English vacationers come here in droves (many have holidayed here annually for decades). The town is filled with pubs that try to help British guests feel right at home.

Pubs and Clubs

The English Inn offers both a street-side pub and a more refined-feeling garden out back—at least until the evening, when the stereo starts blaring. Order up baked beans on toast, fish-and-chips, or just a draft beer (daily, 8:30 until after midnight, Corso Italia 55, tel. 081-807-4357).

Photo offers a snapshot of contemporary Italy with a creative food and drink menu, DJ music, and people-watching among stylish Italians on vacation (described later, under "Eating in Sorrento").

The **Foreigners' Club** offers live Neapolitan songs, Sinatra-style classics, and jazzy elevator-type music nightly at 20:00 throughout the summer. It's just right for old-timers feeling frisky (in the center; described earlier under "Helpful Hints").

Theater Show

At **Teatro Tasso,** a hardworking troupe puts on *The Sorrento Musical,* a folk-music show that treats visitors to a schmaltzy dose of Neapolitan Tarantella music and dance—complete with "Funiculì Funiculà" and "Santa Loo-chee-yee-yah." The 75-minute Italian-language extravaganza features a cast of 14 playing guitar, violin, mandolin, and tambourines, and singing operatically from Neapolitan balconies...with Vesuvius erupting in the background. Your ticket includes a drink before and after the show. While tickets normally cost €25, Maurizio promises my readers tickets for €20 in 2012. He also offers readers a €40 dinner package (normally €50) that includes a four-course meal, drinks, and a seat at the show (discounts good only if you buy tickets directly from their box office and show this book, maximum 2 tickets or dinner packages per book; the earlier in the day you reserve, the better your seats; nightly April-Oct at 21:30, box office and bar open 45 minutes before show, dinner starts at 20:00 and must be reserved in advance, theater seats 350, facing Piazza Sant'Antonino in the old town, tel. 081-807-5525, info@teatrotasso.com).

Sleeping in Sorrento

Hotels here often charge the same for a room whether it has a view, balcony, or neither. At hotels that offer sea views, ask for a room *"con balcone, con vista sul mare"* (with a balcony, with a sea view). *"Tranquillo"* is taken as a request for a quieter room off the street. Hotels listed are either near the train station and city center or along the way to Punta del Capo, a 20-minute walk—or short bus ride—from the station. While many hotels close for the winter, you should have no trouble finding a room any time except in August, when the town is jammed and many hotel prices go way up. Most hotels have two rates: high season (April-Oct) and low. Outside of summer, prices can be soft—it doesn't hurt to ask for a discount (always show this book). Splurge for a hotel with air-conditioning if you wilt in the heat, but be aware that it often costs extra. Note: The spindly, more exotic, and more tranquil Amalfi Coast town of Positano (see next chapter) is also a good place to spend the night.

East of the Center

To reach these hotels, head a block in front of the train station, turn right onto Corso Italia, then left down Via Capasso (which eventually winds right and becomes Via Califano).

$$$ Grand Hotel Ambasciatori is a sumptuous four-star hotel with 100 rooms, a cliffside setting, a sprawling garden, and a pool. This is Humphrey Bogart land, with plush public spaces, a relaxing stay-a-while ambience, and a free elevator to its "private beach"—actually a sundeck built out over the water (viewless

---

Sleep Code

(€1 = about $1.40, country code: 39)
S = Single, **D** = Double/Twin, **T** = Triple, **Q** = Quad, **b** = bathroom, **s** = shower only. Unless otherwise noted, credit cards are accepted, English is spoken, and breakfast is included.

To help you sort easily through these listings, I've divided the accommodations into three categories based on the price for a standard double room with bath:

   $$$ Higher Priced—Most rooms €140 or more.
     $$ Moderately Priced—Most rooms between €80-140.
       $ Lower Priced—Most rooms €80 or less.

Prices can change without notice; verify the hotel's current rates online or by email. For other updates, see www .ricksteves.com/update.

Db-€150, sea-view Db-€350, 10 percent discount with this book or check website for specials, prices vary wildly, air-con in summer, balconies, pay Internet access, parking-€20/day, closed Nov-March, Via Califano 18, tel. 081-878-2025, fax 081-807-1021, www.ambasciatorisorrento.com, ambasciatori@manniello hotels.com).

$$$ Hotel La Meridiana Sorrento, a fine three-star option with everything but character, offers business-class public spaces and 45 soulless rooms, including some with views (Db-€160, Tb-€190, Qb-€240, discounts often available, air-con, elevator, big rooftop terrace with grand views, next door to public Lemon Grove Garden at Via Rota 1, tel. 081-807-3535, fax 081-807-3484, www.lameridianasorrento.com, info@lameridianasorrento.com).

In the Town Center

$$$ Hotel Antiche Mura, with 50 rooms and four stars, is sophisticated, elegant, and plush, offering all the amenities you could need in a hotel. Surrounded by lemon trees, the pool and sundeck are an oasis. Just a block off the main square, it's cheaper than other hotels nearby, and quieter too because it faces a ravine (small-windowed Db-€150, Db-€189, balcony Db-€250; Michele promises 15 percent off in 2012 if you reserve direct, mention this book, and pay cash; about a third cheaper Nov-March, opulent buffet breakfast, air-con, elevator, Wi-Fi, parking-€10/day, a block inland from Piazza Tasso at Via Fuorimura 7, tel. 081-807-3523, fax 081-807-1323, www.hotelantichemura.com, info@hotel antichemura.com).

$$ Casa Astarita B&B is a shining gem in the middle of town, with a crazy-quilt-tiled entryway. You'll find six bright, tranquil air-conditioned rooms (three with little balconies) and a fully stocked communal fridge and sideboard for help-yourself breakfasts in the rustic-yet-elegant common room. Despite double-paned windows, pub noise can seep into some rooms (Db-€95-110, Tb-€130, mention this book for these rates, Wi-Fi, 30 yards past the cathedral on Corso Italia at #67, tel. 081-877-4906, fax 081-877-3991, www.casastarita.com, info@casastarita.com, Annamaria). If there's no one at reception, check in at their shop next door, "Living Casa Astarita," or at Hotel Mignon Meublè (described next)—the same family runs both hotels.

$$ Hotel Mignon Meublè rents 24 soothing blue rooms in a central location near the cathedral (Sb-€80, Db-€105, Tb-€130, these prices good with this book when you reserve direct, air-con, Internet access, rooftop sundeck, some balconies but no views; from the cathedral, walk a block up Corso Italia to Via Sersale 9; tel. 081-807-3824, fax 081-877-4348, www.sorrentohotel

mignon.com, info@sorrentohotelmignon.com, Paolo).

$$ Hotel del Corso is a funky Old World three-star hotel with 26 decent rooms. Family-run with few frills, it doesn't get any more central than this (Db-€110, Tb-€150, Qb-€170, email for specials, €10 off-season discount when you mention this book and pay cash, air-con, rooftop sun terrace, self-service laundry, closed Dec-Feb, near Piazza Tasso at Corso Italia 134, tel. 081-807-1016, fax 081-807-3157, www.hoteldelcorso.com, info@hoteldelcorso .com, Luca and Imma).

$$ Il Palazzo Starace B&B, a lesser value than other hotels in this price range, offers seven tidy rooms in a little alley off Corso Italia (opposite Hotel del Corso, listed earlier), one block from Piazza Tasso (Db-€95, family room-€150, 10 percent off with cash and this book in 2012, includes small breakfast at a bar around the corner, air-con, no elevator but a luggage dumbwaiter; ring bell at Via Santa Maria della Pietà 9, then climb 3 floors; tel. 081-878-4031, mobile 338-276-1418, fax 081-532-9344, www.palazzo starace.com, info@palazzostarace.com, Giovanna).

$ Ulisse Deluxe Hostel is the best budget deal in town, with public areas that feel more like an elegant hotel than a hostel. The 56 marble-tiled rooms have big private bathrooms, so unless you choose to sleep in its dorm, the only thing hostel-like about this place is the price—it's a great value (Db-€70, Tb-€105, Qb-€140, €25/bunk in 2- to 8-bed single-sex dorm, these rates valid when you mention this book and reserve direct, breakfast-€7, air-con, Wi-Fi in lobby, spa and pool use extra, hostel membership not required, a 5-minute walk from the old-town action at Via del Mare 22, tel. 081-877-4753, fax 081-877-4093, www.ulissedeluxe .com, info@ulissedeluxe.com).

$ Hotel Nice rents 29 simple, cramped rooms with high ceilings 100 yards in front of the train station on the noisy main drag. Alfonso promises that you can have a quiet room—critical at this busy location—if you request it with your booking email (Db-€75, €85 in Aug; extra bed-€20; 10 percent discount when you book direct, mention this book, and pay cash; air-con, elevator, rooftop terrace, Wi-Fi, closed Nov-March, Corso Italia 257, tel. 081-878-1650, fax 081-878-3086, www.hotelnice.it, info @hotelnice.it).

$ Hostel Le Sirene, a tiny hostel four blocks from the train station, offers 50 of the cheapest beds in town (€18/bunk in 8- to 10-bed dorms with bath, Db-€65; includes tiny breakfast, linens, and towels; cash only, hostel membership not required, no curfew, open year-round, elevator, pay Internet access, luggage storage, Via degli Aranci 156, tel. 081-807-2925, fax 081-877-1371, www .hostellesirene.com, info@hostellesirene.com).

With a View on Via Capo

These hotels are outside of town, near the cape (straight out Corso Italia, which turns into Via Capo). Once you're set up, commuting into town on the bus is easy. Hotel Minerva and Albergo Settimo Cielo are my favorite Sorrento splurges, while Hotel Désirée and Hotel Elios are better budget bets. If you're in Sorrento to stay put and luxuriate, these accommodations are perfect (although I'd rather luxuriate in Positano—see next chapter).

Getting to Via Capo: From the city center, it's a 15-minute walk (20 minutes from train station, last part is uphill), a €20 taxi ride, or a cheap bus ride. An occasional Via Capo-bound bus leaves from the train station itself (about every 40 minutes, usually blue or green-and-white SITA buses, direction: Massa, don't take one heading for Positano/Amalfi). Many more buses leave from Piazza Tasso in the city center, a five-minute walk from the station (go down a block and turn left on Corso Italia; from far side of the piazza, look for red-and-white bus #A, about 3/hour). Tickets for either bus are sold at the station newsstand and tobacco shops (€2.40). Most Via Capo hotels are near the Hotel Belair bus stop. If you're headed to Via Capo after 19:30, when the center (and Piazza Tasso bus stop) is closed to traffic, catch the bus instead on Via degli Aranci (with your back to the station, wind left, up and around it; the bus stop is near Bar Paradise).

Getting from Via Capo into Town: Buses work great once you get the hang of them (and it's particularly gratifying to avoid the taxi racket). To reach downtown Sorrento from Via Capo, catch any bus heading downhill from Hotel Belair (3/hour, buses run all day and evening).

$$$ Hotel Minerva is like a sun-worshipper's temple. Catch the elevator at Via Capo 32. Getting off on the fifth floor, you'll step onto a spectacular terrace with outrageous Mediterranean views and a small cliff-hanging swimming pool and a cold-water Jacuzzi *con vista*—all complementing 60 large, tiled *limoncello* rooms (Db-€160, Tb-€185, Qb-€210, these discounted prices promised with this book through 2012 only if mentioned when you reserve, air-con, pay Wi-Fi, parking-€15/day, Via Capo 30, tel. 081-878-1011, fax 081-878-1949, www.minervasorrento.com, minerva@acampora.it).

$$$ Hotel La Tonnarella is an old-time Sorrentine villa with several terraces, stylish tiles, and indifferent service. Eighteen of its 24 rooms have views of the sea (non-view Db-€144, sea-view or balcony Db-€180, Db with view terrace-€216, exotic view suite with terrace-€315, email for best rates, €30/person half-pension available, air-con, Internet access and Wi-Fi, small beach with elevator access, closed Dec-Feb, Via Capo 31, tel. 081-878-1153, fax 081-878-2169, www.latonnarella.it, info@latonnarella.it).

$$$ Albergo Settimo Cielo, the aptly named "Seventh Heaven," offers all the views and lazy resort trappings you could want, and is run by a family that really hustles to provide a fine value. At this old-fashioned cliff-hanger sitting 300 steps above Marina Grande, the reception is just off the waterfront side of the road, and the elevator passes down through four floors with 50 dated but clean-and-comfortable rooms—all with grand views, and many with balconies (Sb-€120, Db-€140, Tb-€180, Qb-€215, check website for specials or ask for 5 percent discount on these rates in 2012 when you mention this book when reserving, air-con in summer, Wi-Fi, free parking, inviting pool in the summer, sun terrace, Via Capo 27, tel. 081-878-1012, fax 081-807-3290, www .hotelsettimocielo.com, info@hotelsettimocielo.com, Giuseppe, sons Stefano and Massimo, and daughter Serena).

$$ Hotel Désirée is a modest affair, with humbler vistas but no traffic noise. The 22 basic rooms have high, ravine-facing or partial-sea views, and half come with balconies (all same price). Most rooms have fans, and there's a fine rooftop sunning terrace and lovable cats. Eco-friendly Corinna, daughter Cassandra, and staff—Antonio and Marco—are hugely helpful with tips on exploring the peninsula (Sb-€60, small Db-€75, Db-€85, Tb-€105, Qb-€115, Wi-Fi, laundry-€8, free parking, shares driveway and beach access with La Tonnarella, Via Capo 31, tel. & fax 081-878-1563, www .desireehotelsorrento.com, info@desireehotelsorrento.com).

$ Hotel Elios, warmly run by Gianna, is humble...much like a Sorrentine *nonna*'s house. It offers 14 simple but spacious rooms—12 with balconies and views—a panoramic sun terrace, and a quiet atmosphere. They don't serve breakfast, but you're welcome to use the kitchen and dining room (Sb-€50, Db-€80, Tb-€100, extra bed-€20, family rooms, cheaper off-season, cash only, free parking, closed Dec-March, Via Capo 33, tel. 081-878-1812, www .hotelelios.it, info@hotelelios.it).

Eating in Sorrento

Gourmet Splurges Downtown

In a town proud to have no McDonald's, consider eating well for a few extra bucks. Both of these places are worthwhile splurges run by a hands-on boss with a passion for good food and exacting service. Be prepared to relax and stay a while.

Ristorante il Buco, once the cellar of an old monastery, is now a small, dressy restaurant that serves delightfully presented, playful, and creative modern dishes under a grand, rustic arch. Peppe and his staff love to explain exactly what's on the plate. The dashing team of cooks builds sophisticated dishes in a state-of-the-art kitchen, while a plasma-screen TV shows all the action.

Peppe, who holds the only Michelin star in town, designs his menu around whatever's fresh, and travels in the winter to assemble a wine list sure to offer connoisseurs something new and memorable. Reservations are usually necessary to sit inside under their elegant vault (€18 pastas, €25 *secondi*, dinners run from about €50 plus wine, 10 percent discount when you show this book in 2012, always a good vegetarian selection, extravagant tasting *menu*, Thu-Tue 12:00-15:00 & 19:00-23:00, closed Wed and Jan; just off Piazza Sant'Antonino—facing the basilica, go under the grand arch on the left and immediately enter the restaurant at II Rampa Marina Piccola 5; tel. 081-878-2354).

L'Antica Trattoria serves more traditional cuisine from an inviting menu in a *romantico* candlelit ambience. Run by the same family since 1930, the restaurant has a trellised garden outside and intimate nooks inside (ideal for small groups). Walk around the labyrinthine interior before you select a place to sit. Aldo and sons will take care of you, while the Joe Cocker-esque resident mandolin player entertains. Their wine list features well-known wines from the region. They offer several fixed-price meals—including a €15 two-course lunch and a €46 four-course dinner—or you can order à la carte (€15 pastas, €25 *secondi*, 10 percent discount when you show this book in 2012, vegetarian options, daily 12:00-23:30, closed Mon Nov-Feb, air-con, reservations smart, Via Padre R. Giuliani 33, tel. 081-807-1082).

Eating Well and Cheaply Downtown

Inn Bufalito, which focuses on regional specialties, backs up its motto: "Eating well is for everyone." In an informal setting, Franco and his staff serve up a changing menu of pizza, pasta, and all things buffalo, including a delicious selection of *mozzarella di bufala* (€7 salads, €8 pasta, no cover charge, daily 12:00-24:00, closed Tue off-season and all weekdays Jan-Feb, Vico I Fuoro 21, tel. 081-365-6975).

Photo, a sleek and modern place, has a creative menu, secluded garden, and DJ music. Less traditional and more expensive, it's fun for a drink or a unique meal (May-Nov daily 18:00-late, Dec-April open Fri-Sat only, reservations smart, Via Correale 19, 4-minute walk from Piazza Tasso, tel. 081-877-3686).

Ristorante Pizzeria da Gigino, lively and congested, makes huge, tasty Neapolitan-style pizzas in their wood-burning oven (pizza, pasta, and *secondi* all €8-12 each; daily 12:00-24:00, closed Jan-Feb; just off Piazza Sant'Antonino—take first road to the left of Sant'Antonino as you face him, pass under the archway, and take the first left to Via degli Archi 15; tel. 081-878-1927, Antonino).

Ristorante Pizzeria Lanterna Due offers an agreeable family-run atmosphere celebrating the "food, art, and music of Italian cooking," with a fun staff and decent food. Join the other tourists at the long line of tables along the alley, or in the air-conditioned interior (€8 pastas, €10 *secondi,* daily 12:00-15:30 & 18:00-23:00, Via Santa Maria delle Grazie 28, tel. 081-807-4521).

Meating, as its name implies, focuses on top-quality meats, from homemade sausages to giant steaks. You'll find no seafood or pasta here, but there are a variety of vegetable dishes and delicious local cheeses, along with a reasonably priced selection of wine (€15 steaks, daily 11:30-15:00 & 18:30-24:00, closed Wed off-season, Via della Pietà 20, tel. 081-878-2891).

Pizzeria da Franco seems to be Sorrento's favorite place for basic, casual pizza in a fun, untouristy atmosphere. There's nothing fancy about this place—just locals on benches eating hot sandwiches and great pizzas served on waxed paper in a square tin. It's packed to the rafters with a youthful crowd that doesn't mind the plastic cups (€7 pizzas, €5 salads, daily 12:00-2:00 in the morning, just across from Lemon Grove Garden on busy Corso Italia at #265, tel. 081-877-2066).

Picnics: Markets and take-out pizzerias abound in the old town. If you fancy a picnic dinner on your balcony, on the hotel terrace, or in the Lemon Grove Garden, get a pizza to go at Pizzeria da Franco (listed above) or groceries at the **Standa supermarket** (Mon-Sat 8:30-13:20 & 16:00-20:15, Sun 9:30-13:00 & 17:00-20:30, Corso Italia 223).

Gelato: A few doors downhill from L'Antica Trattoria, **Davide Gelato** has many repeat customers (so many flavors, so little time). In 1957, Augusto Davide opened the shop, and his grandson, Giovanni, proudly carries on the tradition today (look toward the back, where the gelato is made on-site). Walk the most enticing chorus line in Italy before ordering. Sample *Profumi di Sorrento* (an explosive sorbet of mixed fruits) and lemon crème. They also serve simple meals at fair prices (daily 9:30-24:00, shorter hours off-season, closed Nov-March, 2 blocks off Corso Italia at Via Padre R. Giuliani 39, tel. 081-878-1337).

At **Gelateria Primavera,** another local favorite, Antonio and Alberta whip up 70 exotic flavors—and still have time to make pastries for the pope (and everybody else—check out the photos). Try the *noce* (pronounced no-CHAY), made from local walnuts (€3 for up to three flavors, daily 9:00-2:00 in the morning, just west of Piazza Tasso at Corso Italia 142, tel. 081-807-3252).

Dinner with Sea Views

For a decent dinner *con vista,* head for a view terrace at one of these restaurants. To get to Marina Grande, where the first two are located, follow the directions from the cliffside square on the "Welcome to Sorrento" walk (described earlier). For a less scenic route, walk down Via del Mare, past the recommended Ulisse Deluxe Hostel, to the harbor. Either way, it's about a 15-minute stroll from downtown. You can also take bus #D from Piazza Tasso (€2.40).

Ristorante Delfino gets their seafood right off the fishermen's boats at Marina Grande, and serves it up in big portions to hungry locals in a quiet and bright pier restaurant. The cooking, service, and setting are all top-notch, and the prices are good. The restaurant is lovingly run by Luisa, her brothers Andrea and Roberto, and her husband Antonio. They take good care of their guests and give travelers who carry this book a little glass of *limoncello* to cap the experience. If you're here for lunch, take advantage of the wonderful sundeck—show this book to get an hour of relaxation and digestion on the lounge chairs (daily 11:30-15:30 & 18:30-22:30, closed Nov-March; at Marina Grande, facing the water, go all the way to the left and follow signs; tel. 081-878-2038).

Trattoria da Emilia, on the tranquil Marina Grande waterfront, is considerably more rustic, less expensive, and good for straightforward, typical Sorrentine home-cooking, including fresh fish and *gnocchi di mamma*—potato dumplings with meat sauce, basil, and mozzarella (daily 12:15-15:00 & 19:00-22:30, closed Tue Nov-Feb, no reservations taken, indoor and outdoor pier seating, cash only, tel. 081-807-2720).

The **Foreigners' Club Restaurant** has the best sea views in town (under breezy palms), live music nightly at 20:00 (May-Oct), and passable meals. It's a good spot for dessert or an after-dinner *limoncello* (daily, bar opens at 9:30, meals served 11:00-23:00, Via Luigi de Maio 35, tel. 081-877-3263).

On Via Capo
Verde Mare is the locals' pick for a cheaper place (Thu-Tue 12:30-14:45 & 19:00-23:30, closed Wed, 300 yards uphill from La Tonnarella and other recommended hotels, tel. 081-878-2589).

Sorrento Connections

It's impressively fast to zip by boat from Sorrento to most coastal towns and islands during the summer, when there are many more departures. In fact, it's quicker and easier for residents to get around by fast boat than by car or train.

By Train and Bus
From Sorrento to Naples, Pompeii, and Herculaneum by Circumvesuviana Train: This commuter train runs about every 30 minutes between Naples and Sorrento (less frequently on holi-

days, www.vesuviana.it). From Sorrento, it's about 30 minutes to Pompeii, 45 minutes to Herculaneum (€2.10 one-way for either trip), and 70 minutes to Naples (€4 one-way). There's no round-trip discount and all-day passes are generally not worthwhile (except on weekends when they're roughly half-price). If there's a line at the train station, you can also buy tickets at the appropriately-named Snack Bar (across from the main ticket office) or downstairs at the newsstand.

When returning to Naples' Centrale Station on the Circumvesuviana, get off at the next-to-the-last station, Garibaldi (Centrale station is just up the escalator). Bonus: When returning from Sorrento, your Circumvesuviana ticket includes travel on the Naples Metro or bus system within three hours of validation (no need to validate again). The trip is also covered by the Campania ArteCard. The schedule is printed in the free *Surrentum* magazine (available at TI). Note that the risk of theft is mostly limited to suburban Naples, but can be a problem anywhere. Going between Sorrento and Pompeii or Herculaneum is generally safer.

From Sorrento to the Naples Airport: Six Curreri buses run daily to and from the airport; confirm the schedule at the TI (€10, pay driver, daily at 6:30, 8:30, 10:30, 12:00, 14:00, and 16:30, may be more in summer—double-check the schedule, 1.5 hours, departs from in front of train station, tel. 081-801-5420, www .curreriviaggi.it).

To the Amalfi Coast: See page 84.

To Rome: Most people ride the Circumvesuviana 70 minutes to Naples, then catch the express train to Rome. However, the direct Sorrento-Rome bus is cheaper, and can actually be more convenient. Marozzi buses leave Sorrento's train station daily for Rome's Tiburtina station (€17.50, Mon-Sat at 6:00 and 17:00, Sun at 17:00, off-season at 6:00 only, 4 hours; buy tickets by phone, at some travel agencies, or on board for a €4 surcharge; also stops at Pompei Scavi and Naples' Port Beverello, tel. 080-579-0111, www.marozzivt.it). A Curreri bus makes the trip as well (€16, departs Mon-Sat at 6:30, 4 hours, tel. 081-801-5420, www.curreriviaggi.it).

By Boat

The number of boats that run per day varies according to the season. The frequency indicated here is for roughly mid-May through mid-October, with more boats per day in summer and fewer off-season. Check all schedules with the TI, your hotel, or online (visit the individual boat company websites—see below—or visit www.capritourism.com, select English, and click on "Shipping timetable"). The Caremar line, a subsidized state-run ferry company, takes cars, offers fewer departures, and is just a bit slower—

but cheaper—than the other boat. All of the boats take several hundred people each—and frequently fill up.

From Sorrento to Capri: Boats run at least hourly. Your options include a fast **ferry** (*traghetto* or *nave veloce*, 4/day, 25 minutes, €9.80, run by Caremar, tel. 081-807-3077, www.caremar.it) or a faster but pricier **jet boat** (*aliscafi*, 18/day, 20 minutes, €14, run by Gescab, tel. 081-807-1812, www.gescab.it). To minimize the crowds on Capri, it's best to buy your ticket at 8:00 and take the 8:25 jet boat (if you miss it, try to depart by 9:30 at the very latest). These early boats can be jammed, but it's worth it once you reach the island.

From Sorrento to Other Points: Naples (6/day, departs roughly every 2 hours, 35 minutes, €10; starting at 9:00), **Positano** (mid-April-mid-Oct only, 2-4/day, 40 minutes, €11), **Amalfi** (mid-April-mid-Oct only, 2-4/day, 1.25 hours, €12). For a slightly less touristy alternative to Capri, consider the nearby island of **Ischia** (1/day, Easter-Nov only, departure usually around 9:30, more frequent from Naples, 1 hour, €32 round-trip).

Getting to Sorrento's Port: To get from Sorrento's Piazza Tasso to Marina Piccola (the port), walk down the stairs near the statue's left side (about 10 minutes), or take the slightly longer road (with fewer stairs) that passes by the TI and Foreigners' Club. Or, from Piazza Sant'Antonino, catch a red-and-white bus #B or #C (3/hour, €1, buy ticket at tobacco shop and specify that you're going to the *porto*) or the little blue bus (4/hour, €1, buy ticket from driver). Boat tickets are sold only at the port.

Capri

Capri was made famous as the vacation hideaway of Roman emperors Augustus and Tiberius. In the 19th century, it was the haunt of Romantic Age aristocrats on their Grand Tour of Europe. But these days, the island is a world-class tourist trap, packed with gawky name tag-wearing visitors searching for the rich and famous, and finding only their prices.

The "Island of Dreams" is a zoo in July and August— overrun with tacky, low-grade group tourism at its worst. Other times of year,

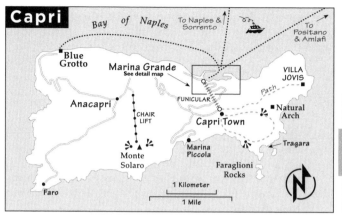

while still crowded, it can provide a relaxing and scenic break from the cultural gauntlet of Italy.

Planning Your Time

This is the best see-everything-in-a-day plan from Sorrento: Take an early jet boat to Capri (buy ticket at 8:00, boat leaves at 8:25 and arrives at 8:45—smart). Go directly to the Blue Grotto, then catch a bus from the grotto to Anacapri and ride the chairlift to Monte Solaro. From the summit, return by chairlift (or hike down). Stroll out from the base of the chairlift to Villa San Michele for the view, then catch a bus to Capri town for the rest of your stay. At the end of the day, ride the funicular down to Marina Grande (kill time lazing on the free beach or wandering the yacht harbor) to catch the boat back to Sorrento.

Efficient travelers can make a quick trip here between destinations: Sail from Sorrento, check your bag at the harbor, see Capri, and boat directly from here to Naples.

If you buy a one-way ticket to Capri (there's no round-trip discount), you'll have maximum schedule flexibility and can take either the ferry or the jet boat back. (Check times for the last return crossing upon arrival; on Capri, get a schedule from the TI or check at boat-ticket kiosk or automated boat-departure board.) During July and August, however, it's wise to get a round-trip boat ticket with a late return (improving your odds of getting a spot on a boat when they're most crowded)—and you can use the ticket to return earlier if you like. Be 20 minutes early for the boat, or you can be bumped.

Day-trippers come down from Rome, creating a daily rush hour in each direction (arriving between 10:00-11:00, leaving around 17:00). The trip to the Blue Grotto is just a 20-minute boat ride from the arrival dock, but the commotion there can amount to a two-hour delay. If you're heading to Capri specifically to see the Blue Grotto, be sure to check that the tide isn't too high or the water too rough—ask the TI or your hotelier before heading over.

Orientation to Capri

First thing—pronounce it right: KAH-pree, not kah-PREE like the song or the pants. The island is small—just four miles by two miles—and is separated from the Sorrento Peninsula by a narrow strait. Home to 13,000 people, there are only two towns to speak of: Capri and Anacapri. The island also has some scant Roman ruins and a few interesting churches and villas. But its chief attraction is its famous Blue Grotto, and its best activity is a chairlift up the island's Monte Solaro.

Arrival in Capri

Get oriented on the boat before you dock. As you near the harbor, Capri spreads out before you: The port is called **Marina Grande** (TI, boats to Blue Grotto, buses to anywhere, funicular to the town of Capri). **Capri town** fills the ridge high above the harbor. The ruins of Emperor Tiberius' palace, **Villa Jovis,** cap the peak on the left. The dramatic *"Mamma mia!"* road arcs around the highest mountain on the island **(Monte Solaro)** on the right, leading up to **Anacapri** (the island's second town, just out of sight). Notice the old zigzag steps below that road. Until 1874, this was the only connection between Capri and Anacapri. (Though it's quite old, it's nowhere near as old as its nickname, "The Phoenician Stairway," implies.) The white house on the ridge above the zigzags is **Villa San Michele** (where you can go later for a grand view of boats like the one you're on now).

Upon arrival, get your bearings. Boats dock in two places: on the long pier and directly by the main street. If your boat arrives on the main street, take a right to get to the long pier. Stand with your back to the pier: The **funicular** is across the street. The fourth little shop to the right of the funicular (no sign, sells clothes and souvenirs) provides **baggage storage** in the back of the store (€3/ day per bag, daily 9:00-18:00, tel. 081-837-4575). If it's closed, try the upper funicular station in Capri town (€3/bag, daily 7:00-20:00; be aware that you may have to pay extra to take big bags up the funicular). The kiosk that sells **bus and funicular tickets** is to your right, in the cluster of buildings at the start of the pier. Behind that are kiosks that sell return **boat tickets** (for the two competing companies). Across the street and uphill from all this are the **public WCs.**

The **TI** is near the ticket kiosk, right by the stubby dock for Blue Grotto boats (April-Oct Mon-Sat 9:15-13:15 & 15:00-18:15,

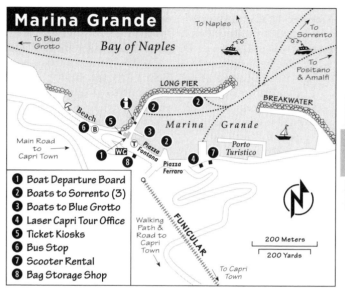

Sun 9:00-15:00, shorter hours off-season; pick up free map—or the better €1 map if you'll be venturing to the outskirts of Capri town or Anacapri, tel. 081-837-0634, www.capritourism.com).

From the port, you have several transit options: boat to the Blue Grotto (best early—ideally upon arrival), bus to Capri town or Anacapri (often with long and frustrating lines), or funicular up to Capri town (4/hour, 5 minutes). If you have energy to burn, a steep paved footpath connects the port area with Capri town. It starts a block inland from the ferry dock, near the Laser Capri office (follow the signs to *Capri centro*; allow 30 minutes).

Helpful Hints

Cheap Tricks: A cheap day trip to Capri is tough. From Sorrento to Capri by boat costs from €9.80 to €14 each way, and Blue Grotto tickets (plus transportation) come to €23.50—that's about €45-55 per person. Taking the bus rather than the boat to the Blue Grotto (see next page) saves about €9 per person. Although technically illegal, after the boats stop running, anyone can see the Blue Grotto for free, if you're willing to swim in.

Best Real Hike: Serious hikers love the peaceful and scenic three-hour Fortress Hike, which takes you entirely away from the tourists. You'll walk under ruined forts along the rugged coast, from the Blue Grotto to the *faro* (lighthouse). From there, you can take a bus back to Anacapri (3/hour). The tourist office has a fine map/brochure.

Free Beach: Marina Grande has a free pebbly beach. You can get a shower at the bar for €1.

Local Guide: Giovanna Donadio is a good tour guide for Sorrento, Amalfi, and Capri (€100/half-day, €160/day, same price for any size group, mobile 338-466-0114, giovanna _dona@hotmail.com). **Pina Esposito** also does tours of the entire region (confirm one week in advance, sometimes available on shorter notice, mobile 349-596-8251, annamaria esposito1@virgilio.it).

Boat Departure Schedule: A very handy electronic board lists all boats departing in the next hour or so from Capri. It's on the end of the building between the TI and boat-ticket kiosk (on the wall facing the mainland). This is the one way to know all the departure options coming up and to confirm your boat's departure time and dock number. The board includes a small chart that locates the many dock numbers in this confusing harbor.

Getting Around Capri

The buses and funicular are covered by the same ticket options: €1.40 per ride (two single tickets are the easiest option if going straight to Blue Grotto by public bus—one to get to Anacapri, then one to get to the Blue Grotto) or €7.90 for an all-day pass (includes deposit, turn it in at the end of the day to get €1 back). Single-ride tickets are often available at newsstands, tobacco shops, or from the driver. All-day passes and funicular tickets are usually sold only at official ticket offices. Consider an all-day pass if you plan to take more than five rides on the buses and funicular (possible if you go by bus to the Blue Grotto and spend some time in each town). Schedules are clearly posted at all bus stations. Taxis have steep and fixed rates (Marina Grande to Capri-€15; Marina Grande to Anacapri-€20). You can hire a taxi for about €70 per hour—negotiate.

Buses and Funicular from the Port at Marina Grande: Buses pick up just uphill from the ticket booth (you can also buy tickets from driver). Get in line under the appropriate sign: either under *San Costanzo* for going up to the town of **Capri** (at least 4/ hour, 10 minutes), where you could then transfer to Anacapri (4/ hour, 10 minutes, often a long queue for this Capri-Anacapri bus); or direct to **Anacapri** (sporadic schedule, but about every 40 minutes, 25 minutes). For most people, the best way from the port to Anacapri is to take the funicular to Capri (4/hour, on the quarter-hour, 5 minutes; if there's a long line, the bus might be quicker), and then bus from there to Anacapri.

Buses from Anacapri: To use the buses intelligently in Anacapri, you need to know that there are two stops: the town center (Piazza Vittoria) and the cemetery stop (Piazza della Pace—pronounced "PAH-chay"—just 200 yards farther down the main road; residents may refer to it by its former name, Piazza del Cimitero). Buses to **Capri town** (at least 4/hour) and the port, **Marina Grande** (less frequent), can be packed. Guarantee a place by catching the bus from the Piazza della Pace stop, one stop before most people get on (for either destination, catch the bus on the street corner across from the newsstand). Anacapri-Blue Grotto buses depart only from the Piazza della Pace stop (not from the town center). If you're coming from the town of Capri and want to transfer to the **Blue Grotto** buses, don't get off when the driver announces "Anacapri." Instead, ride one more stop to Piazza della Pace, then transfer to the Grotta Azzurra (Blue Grotto) bus (3/hour, 10 minutes). If in doubt, ask the driver or a local.

Boat Trips Around the Island: Laser Capri runs quick trips around the island, passing stunning cliffs, caves, and views that most miss when they go only to the Blue Grotto. If you have an hour, it's well worth the extra €3. Their tiny ticket window faces dock #23 at Marina Grande, from where its boats offer three excursions: circle the island without grotto stop (1 hour, €15); circle the island with a grotto stop (2 hours, €15); and just to the grotto and back (about 1 hour, €12). The €11.50 grotto admission is always extra (boats leave daily from 9:00 until an hour before sunset, shorter hours off-season, Via Don Giobbe Ruocco 45, tel. 081-837-5208, www.lasercapri.com). Another company, **Motoscafisti Capri,** offers the grotto trip for the same price.

Scooter Rental: If you like riding a scooter, this is the perfect way to have the run of the island—although the steep and narrow roads aren't ideal for novice riders. **Ciro** proudly rents 40 bright-yellow scooters with 50cc engines—strong enough to haul couples. Rental includes a map and instructions with parking tips and other helpful information (€15/hour, €55/day, €5 discount with this book for 2 hours or more in 2012; includes helmet, gas, and insurance; daily 9:30-19:00, look for the Ferrari sign at Via Don Giobbe Ruocco 55, Marina Grande, tel. 081-837-8018, mobile 338-360-6918, www.capriscooter.com).

Sights in Capri

Capri Town

This is a cute but extremely touristy shopping town. The *funiculare* drops you just around the corner from Piazza Umberto, the town's main square. The **TI** fills a closet under the bell tower on Piazza Umberto (less crowded than its sister on the port: Mon-Sat 9:00-13:00 & 16:00-19:15, Sun 9:00-15:00, shorter hours off-season,

tel. 081-837-0686, WC and baggage storage downstairs behind TI). With your back to the funicular, the bus stop is 50 yards down Via Roma. The footpath to the port starts just behind the TI near the baggage storage (follow signs to *Il Porto*, 15-minute walk).

Capri's multi-domed Baroque **cathedral,** which faces the square, is worth a quick look. (Its multicolored marble floor at the altar was scavenged from the Emperor Tiberius's villa in the 19th century.)

To the left of City Hall (Municipio, lowest corner), a lane leads into the medieval part of town, which has plenty of eateries and is the starting point for the walk to Villa Jovis. The lane to the left of the cathedral (past Bar Tiberio, under the wide arch) has been dubbed "Rodeo Drive" by residents because it's the fashionable shopping strip. Walk a few minutes down Rodeo Drive (past Gelateria Buonocore at #35, with its tempting fresh waffle cones) to Quisisana Hotel, the island's top old-time hotel. From there, head left for fancy shops and villas, and right for gardens and views. Downhill and to the right, a five-minute walk leads to a lovely public garden, Giardini Augusto (free, daily 9:00-18:30).

Villa Jovis and the Emperor's Capri

Even before becoming emperor, Augustus loved Capri so much that he traded the family-owned Isle of Ischia to the (then-independent) Neapolitans in exchange for making Capri his personal property. Emperor Tiberius spent a decade here, 26-37 A.D. (Some figure he did so in order to escape being assassinated in Rome.)

Emperor Tiberius' ruined villa, Villa Jovis, is a scenic 45-minute hike from Capri town. You won't find any statues or mosaics here—just an evocative, ruined complex of terraces fitting a rocky perch over a sheer drop to the sea...and a lovely view. You can make out a large water reservoir for baths, the foundations of servants' quarters, and Tiberius' private apartments (fragments of marble flooring still survive). The ruined lighthouse dates from the Middle Ages.

Cost and Hours: €2, daily 9:00-19:00, closes earlier off-season, tel. 081-837-4549.

▲▲Blue Grotto

Three thousand tourists a day spend a couple of hours visiting Capri's Blue Grotto (Grotta Azzurra). I did—early (when the

light is best), without the frustration of crowds, and with choppy waves nearly making entrance impossible...and it was great.

The actual cave experience isn't much: a five-minute dinghy ride through a three-foot-high entry hole to reach a 60-yard-long cave, where the sun reflects brilliantly blue

on its limestone bottom. But the experience—getting there, getting in, and getting back—is a scenic hoot. You get a fast ride on a 30-foot boat partway around the gorgeous island; along the way you see bird life and dramatic limestone cliffs with scant narration. You'll understand why Roman emperors appreciated the invulnerability of the island—it's surrounded by cliffs, with only one access point, and therefore easy to defend.

At the grotto's "distribution center," you pile into eight-foot dinghies with other tourists; from there, ruffian rowers elbow their way to the tiny hole, then pull fast and hard on the cable at the low point of the swells to squeeze you into the grotto. Then your man rows you around, spouting off a few descriptive lines and singing "O Sole Mio." Depending upon the strength of the sunshine that day, the blue light inside is brilliant.

The grotto was actually an ancient Roman *nymphaeum*—a retreat for romantic hanky-panky. Many believe that, in its day, a tunnel led here directly from the palace, and that the grotto experience was enlivened by statues of Poseidon and company, placed half-underwater as if emerging from the sea. It was ancient Romans who smoothed out the entry hole that's still used to this day.

Typically, your boatman will extort an extra tip out of you before taking you back outside to your big boat (€1 is enough, but you don't need to pay a penny...you've already paid plenty).

Cost and Logistics: Two companies make the boat trip from Marina Grande—Motoscafisti Capri and Laser Capri (€12 roundtrip, no discount for one-way, daily from 9:00 until an hour before sunset, shorter hours off-season, boats don't run in stormy weather or during high tides—check weather and tide conditions *before* you purchase boat tickets; Motoscafista Capri—tel. 081-837-7714, www.motoscafisticapri.com; Laser Capri—tel. 081-837-5208, www.lasercapri.com).

Once you reach the grotto, you pay €7.50 for a rowboat to take you in for the five-minute row around the inside of the grotto (after your rower jockeys for position for at least 20 minutes), plus €4 to cover the admission to the grotto (€11.50 total for grotto visit, not counting €12 round-trip ride from port; again, tip entirely optional). While technically against the rules, some people dive in for free after the boats stop running—a magical experience and a favorite among locals.

When the waves or high tide make entering dangerous, the boats don't go in—the grotto can close without notice, sending tourists (flush with anticipation) home without a chance to squeeze through the little hole. (If this happens to you, consider the one-hour, €15 boat ride around the island—including a look at the Faraglioni Rocks—offered by both companies.)

You can take the boat back, or request to be dropped off on a small dock next to the grotto to return by bus to Anacapri (no discount for one-way boat ticket, stairs lead to bus stop with posted schedule, roughly 3/hour, 10 minutes, buy ticket from driver, €1.40). If you're on a budget, you can take the bus from Anacapri directly to the grotto (rather than a boat from Marina Grande). You'll save about €9, and see a beautiful, calmer side of the island (every 20 minutes from Piazza della Pace, a 200-yard walk on the main road beyond the Piazza Vittoria bus stop in Anacapri).

If you're coming from Capri's port, allow 1-3 hours for the entire visit, depending on the chaos at the caves (an early trip will get you there at the same time as the boatmen in their dinghies—who hitch a ride behind your boat—resulting in less chaos and a shorter wait at the entry point).

Anacapri

Capri's second town has no sea views but some fun and interesting activities. From the busy Piazza Vittoria, where the bus drops you, head to the right of the statue of "Anacapri," and go 40 yards down the pedestrian street Via Orlandi to reach the tiny **TI** (Mon-Sat 9:00-15:00, closed Sun, often closed Nov-Easter, Via Orlandi 59, tel. 081-837-1524). Walk on this street for another ten minutes or so, passing the Casa Rossa, St. Michael's Church, shops, and peaceful side streets. You'll also find a number of eateries, including a couple of good choices for quick, inexpensive pizza, panini, and other goodies: **Sciué Sciué** (informal seating or take-away, daily April-Nov, closed Dec-March, near the TI at #73, tel. 081-837-2068) and **Pizza e Pasta** (take-away only, daily March-Dec, closed Jan-Feb, just before the church at #157, tel. 328-623-8460).

For a sweeping island view just a few minutes away, go to the top of the stairs in Piazza Vittoria, and take the pedestrian path that heads left, past the deluxe Capri Palace Hotel (venture in if you can get past the treacherously eye-catching swimming pool windows), and below the Villa San Michele. (The view is even better from the villa—described next.)

Villa San Michele—The 19th-century mansion of Axel Munthe, Capri's grand personality, offers an insight into the scene here when this was the only comfortable refuge for Europe's artsy gay community. Oscar Wilde, D. H. Lawrence, and company hung out here back when being gay could land you in jail...or worse. Munthe, a Swedish doctor who lived here until 1949, left this impressive mansion littered with Roman statues, the Olivetum (museum of native birds and bugs), and a delightful garden. From the sphinx, you'll enjoy one of Capri's best views.

Cost and Hours: €6, daily 9:00-18:00, closes earlier off-season, tel. 081-837-1401, www.villasanmichele.eu.

Casa Rossa (Red House)—This "Pompeiian-red," eccentric home is a hodgepodge of architectural styles, and the former residence of a Confederate colonel who moved to Capri after the American Civil War. Its small collection of 19th-century paintings of scenes from around the island recalls a time before mass tourism. Don't miss the top floor, with its three scarred ancient statues, which were recovered from the depths of the Blue Grotto in 1964.

Cost and Hours: €3; free with ticket stub from Blue Grotto, Villa San Michele, or Monte Solaro chairlift; June-Sept Tue-Sun 10:00-13:30 & 17:30-20:00, closed Mon; April-May and Oct Tue-Sun 10:00-17:00, closed Mon; closed Nov-March, Via Orlandi 78, tel. 081-838-2193.

▲**St. Michael's Church**—This church has a remarkable majolica floor showing paradise on earth in a classic 18th-century Neapolitan style. The entire floor is ornately tiled, featuring an angel (with flaming sword) driving Adam and Eve from paradise. The devil is wrapped around the trunk of a beautiful tree. The animals—happily ignoring this momentous event—all have human expressions. For the best view, climb the spiral stairs from the postcard desk.

Cost and Hours: €2, daily April-Oct 9:00-19:00, Nov-March 10:00-14:00; in town center—after the TI, continue walking five minutes and look for the signs to *Chiesa Monumentale San Michele*; tel. 081-837-2396.

Faro—The lighthouse is a favorite place to enjoy the sunset, with a private beach, pool, small restaurants, and a few fishermen. Reach it by bus from Anacapri (3/hour, departs from Piazza della Pace stop).

▲▲**Chairlift up to Monte Solaro**—From Anacapri, ride the chairlift to the 1,900-foot summit of Monte Solaro for a commanding view of the Bay of Naples. Work on your tan as you float over hazelnut, walnut, chestnut, apricot, peach, kiwi, and fig trees, past a montage of tourists (mostly from cruise ships; when the grotto is closed—as it often is—they bring passengers here instead). As you ascend, consider how Capri's real estate has been

priced out of the locals' reach. The ride takes 15 minutes each way, and you'll want at least 30 minutes on top.

Cost and Hours: €7.50 one-way, €10 round-trip, daily June-Oct 9:30-17:00, last run down at 17:30, closes earlier Nov-May, confirm schedule with TI, departs from top of the steps in Piazza Vittoria—the first Anacapri bus stop, tel. 081-837-1428.

At the Summit: You'll enjoy the best panorama possible: lush cliffs busy with seagulls enjoying the ideal nesting spot. The Faraglioni Rocks—with tour boats squeezing through every few minutes—are an icon of the island. The pink building nearest the rocks was an American R&R base during World War II. Eisenhower and Churchill met here. On the peak closest to Cape Sorrento, you can see the distant ruins of the Emperor Tiberius' palace, Villa Jovis. Pipes from the Sorrento Peninsula bring water to Capri (demand for fresh water here long ago exceeded the supply provided by the island's three natural springs). The Galli Islands mark the Amalfi Coast in the distance. Cross the bar terrace for views of Mount Vesuvius and Naples.

Hiking Down: A highlight for hardy walkers (provided you have strong knees and good shoes) is the 40-minute downhill hike from the top of Monte Solaro, through lush vegetation and ever-changing views, past the 14th-century Chapel of Santa Maria Cetrella (at the trail's only intersection, it's a 10-minute detour to the right), and back into Anacapri. The trail starts downstairs, past the WCs (last chance). Down two more flights of stairs, look for the sign to *Anacapri e Cetrella*—you're on your way. While the trail is well-established, you'll encounter plenty of uneven steps, loose rocks, and few signs.

Capri Connections

From Capri's Marina Grande by Boat to: Positano (mid-April-mid-Oct, 2-4/day, 35-50 minutes, €15-17; less off-season), **Amalfi** (mid-April-mid-Oct, 2-4/day, 50-75 minutes, €15-17), **Sorrento** (fast ferry: 4/day, 25 minutes, €9.80, jet boat: 18/day, 20 minutes,

€14), **Naples** (roughly 2/hour, 45 minutes, €16), **Salerno** (mid-April-Sept, 2/day, 2 hours, €16). Confirm the schedule carefully—last boats usually leave between 18:00 and 20:10. All departing boats are listed at the port on a handy lighted schedule board, which notes exact dock locations for each departure (facing the taxis, the board is just around the corner from the TI).

AMALFI COAST AND PAESTUM

With its stunning scenery, hill- and harbor-hugging towns, and historic ruins, Amalfi is Italy's coast with the most. The bus trip from Sorrento to Salerno along the breathtaking Amalfi Coast is one of the world's great bus rides. It will leave your mouth open and your camera's memory card full. You'll gain respect for the Italian engineers who built the roads in the 1800s—and even more respect for the bus drivers who drive it today. Cantilevered garages, hotels, and villas cling to the vertical terrain, and beautiful sandy coves tease from far below and out of reach. As you hyperventilate, notice how the Mediterranean, a sheer 500-foot drop below, really twinkles. All this beautiful scenery apparently inspires local Romeos and Juliets, with the evidence of late-night romantic encounters littering the roadside turnouts. Over the centuries, the spectacular scenery and climate have been a siren call for the rich and famous, luring Roman emperor Tiberius, Richard Wagner, Sophia Loren, Gore Vidal, and others to the Amalfi Coast's special brand of *la dolce vita*.

Planning Your Time

On a quick visit, use Sorrento as your home base and do the Amalfi Coast as a day trip. But for a small-town vacation from your vacation, spend a few more days on the coast, perhaps sleeping in Positano or Amalfi town.

Trying to decide between staying in Sorrento, Positano, or Amalfi? Sorrento is the largest of the three, with the best transportation connections. Positano is the most chic and picturesque, with a decent beach. The town of Amalfi has the most actual sights and the best hiking opportunities.

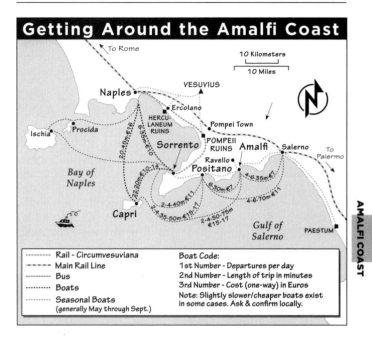

Getting Around the Amalfi Coast

Amalfi Coast towns are pretty but are generally touristy, congested, overpriced, and a long hike above tiny, pebbly beaches. Most beaches are private, and access is expensive. Check and understand your bills in this greedy region. The real thrill here is the scenic Amalfi drive. This is treacherous stuff—even if you have a car, you may want to take the bus or hire a taxi. Brave souls enjoy seeing the coast by scooter or motorbike (rent in Sorrento). The most logical springboard for this trip is Sorrento (see previous chapter), but Positano and Amalfi work, too.

Many travelers do the Amalfi Coast as a round-trip by bus, but a good strategy is to go one way by bus and return by boat. For example, instead of busing from Sorrento to Salerno (end of the line) and back, consider taking the bus to Salerno, then catch-

ing the ferry back to Amalfi or Positano, and from either town, hop a ferry to Sorrento.

Perhaps the simplest option is to take the bus to Positano and boat from there back to Sorrento (or vice-versa). Note that ferry service for this trip decreases or may not exist at all off-season (mid-Oct–mid-April). Boats don't run in stormy weather.

Looking for exercise? Consider an Amalfi Coast hike. Numerous trails connect the main towns along the coast with villages on the hills. Get a good map and/or book before you venture out.

By Bus

From Sorrento: SITA buses depart from Sorrento's train station nearly hourly (in peak season, 20/day, marked *Amalfi via Positano*) and stop at all Amalfi Coast towns (Positano in 50 minutes; Amalfi in another 50 minutes), ending up in Salerno, at the far end of the coast, in about three hours (easy transfer in Amalfi). Ticket prices vary with trip length (45-minute ride, good for trips within the city-€2.40; 1.5-hour ride, good to Positano-€3.60; 24-hour All Amalfi Coast ticket, good to Amalfi and beyond-€7.20; 3-day ticket-€18). For most trips, you'll want the 24-hour All Amalfi Coast ticket. In summer, buses start running as early as 6:30 and run as late as 22:00 (they stop running earlier off-season; check the schedule). Buy tickets at the tobacco shop nearest any bus stop before boarding.

An info booth is across from the bus stop (mid-April-Oct daily 8:30-13:30), but the tobacco shop/newsstand at street level in the train station is more reliable (daily 7:00-13:30 & 14:30-20:00, also sells Circumvesuviana train tickets). If both are closed, try the appropriately-named Snack Bar, upstairs in the station, or Bar Frisby, just down the hill.

Line up under the *Bus Stop SITA* sign (where a schedule is posted on the wall) across from the Sorrento train station (10 steps down). Carefully note the lettered codes that differentiate daily buses from weekend-only buses. *Giornaliero* means daily; *Feriale* notes Monday-Saturday departures; and *Festivo* is for Sundays and holidays. After 19:30 (and occasionally on Sundays—check the sign at the main bus stop), buses may leave from Via degli Aranci (with your back to the station, go left and wind around it; the bus stop is near Bar Paradise).

Leaving Sorrento, grab a seat on the right for the best views. If you return by bus, it's fun to sit directly behind the driver for a box seat with a view over the twisting hairpin action. Sitting toward the front will also minimize carsickness.

Avoiding Crowds on the Bus: Buses are routinely unable to handle the demand during summer months and holidays. Occasionally, an extra bus is added to handle the overflow. Generally, if you don't get on one bus, you're well-positioned to catch the next one (bring a book). Try to arrive early in the morning. Remember that buses start taking off as early as 6:30; and beginning at 8:30, they leave about every 30 minutes. Departures between 9:00 and 11:00 are crowded and frustrating. Count the number of people in line: Buses pull in empty and seat 48 (plus 25 standing).

Returning to Sorrento: The congestion can be so bad in the summer—particularly July and August—that return buses don't even stop in Positano (because they've been filled in Amalfi). Those trying to get back to Sorrento are stuck with taking an extortionist taxi or, if in Positano, hopping a boat...if one's running. If touring the coast by bus, do Positano first and come home from Amalfi to avoid the problem of full buses.

By Boat

Several companies compete for passengers, and usually claim to know nothing about their rivals' services. It's wise to check posted schedules, pick up ferry schedules from the TI, and confirm times to figure out the best plan. The boats servicing Sorrento, Positano, and Amalfi generally operate mid-April through mid-October (pick up schedule at TI, buy ticket on dock). Few boats run off-season.

From Salerno, ferries run from mid-April through September from Piazza Concordia to Amalfi (4-6/day, 35 minutes, €7), continuing to Positano (4-6/day, 70 minutes total, €11; tickets and info at TravelMar, Piazza Concordia, tel. 089-872-950, www.travelmar.it). Salerno's dock is conveniently located at the Amalfi Coast bus stop.

By Taxi

Given the hairy driving, impossible parking, congested buses, and potential fun, you might consider splurging to hire your own car and driver for the Amalfi day. (Don't bother for Pompeii, as the Circumvesuviana train serves it conveniently and only licensed guides can take you into the site.)

The Monetti family—**Raffaele,** brother-in-law **Tony,** and cousin **Lorenzo**—have long taken excellent care of my readers' transportation needs from Sorrento. Sample trips and rates for their comfortable Mercedes taxis: Amalfi Coast Day (Positano-Amalfi

 with time for lunch in Ravello), eight hours, €260; Amalfi Coast and Paestum, 10 hours, €360; transfer to Naples airport or train station, one hour, €110. To get these special prices (promised for up to three people through 2012), mention this book. The Monettis also do other excursions (including pick-up from cruise-ship

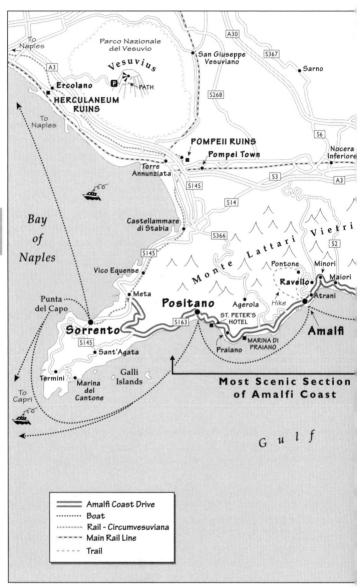

AMALFI COAST

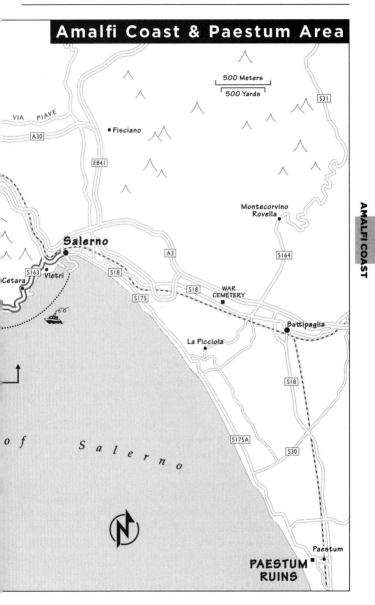

Amalfi Coast & Paestum Area

500 Meters

500 Yards

S31

VIA PIAVE

A30

• Fisciano

E841

Montecorvino
Rovella

Salerno

A3

S164

S163 Vietri

S18

Cetara

S18

S175

S18

WAR
CEMETERY

Battipaglia

La Picciola

S18

of   Salerno

S175A

S30

Paestum

PAESTUM
RUINS

ports) and can take up to eight passengers—at a higher rate schedule—in their air-conditioned Mercedes van. Payment is by cash only. Their reservation system is simple and reliable (Raffaele's mobile 335-602-9158 or 338-946-2860, "office" run by Raffaele's English-speaking wife, Susanna, fax 081-807-4531, www.monettitaxi17.it, monettitaxi17@libero.it).

Be careful: Many cabbies claim to be the Monettis. The real Monettis (Raffaele and Carmello are pictured on page 85) drive Mercedes van-taxi #17, which is usually found at Sorrento's Piazza Tasso. Raffaele's dad, **Carmello** (a jolly, singing, in-love-with-life grandfatherly type who speaks only Italian) occasionally does trips; his specialty is helping Italian Americans find their families in southern Italy. Email him in advance if you want to find your long-lost relatives, and he can put together a meeting and transportation package. If you get in any kind of a jam, call Raffaele's mobile phone for information.

Umberto and Giovanni Benvenuto offer transport and narrated excursions throughout the Amalfi Coast, as well as to Rome, Naples, Pompeii, and more. While as friendly as the Monettis, they're more up-market and formal, with steeper rates explained on their website (tel. 089-874-024, mobile 346-684-0226, www.benvenutolimos.com, info@benvenutolimos.com).

Sorrento Silver Star has professional drivers and several comfortable Mercedes cars and vans, and offers custom trips throughout the region at prices somewhere between the Monettis' and the Benvenutos' (tel. 081-877-1224, mobile 339-388-8143, www.sorrentosilverstar.com, Luisa).

Anthony Buonocore is based in Amalfi but does excursions and transfers anywhere in the region in his more basic but air-conditioned six-person van (rates vary depending on trip, tel. 349-441-0336, www.amalfitransfer.com, buonocoreanthony@yahoo.it).

Rides Only: If you're hiring a cabbie off the street for a ride and not a tour, here are sample fares from Sorrento to Positano: up to four people one-way for about €80 in a car, or up to six people for €90 in a minibus. Figure on paying 50 percent more to Amalfi. While taxis must use a meter within a city, a fixed rate is OK otherwise. Negotiate—ask about a round-trip.

Self-Guided Bus Tour

Hugging the Amalfi Coast

The trip from Sorrento to Salerno is one of the all-time great white-knuckle rides. Gasp from the right side of the bus as you go out and from the left as you return to Sorrento. (Those on the wrong side really miss out.) Traffic is so heavy that private tour buses are

only allowed to go in one direction (southbound from Sorrento)—summer traffic is infuriating. Fluorescent-vested policemen are posted at tough bends during peak hours to help fold in side-view mirrors and keep things moving.

Here's a loosely guided tour of what you're seeing, from west to east (note that many of these towns are described in greater detail later in this chapter):

Leaving Sorrento, the road winds up into the hills past lemon groves and hidden houses. Traveling the coast, you'll see several watchtowers placed within sight of each other, so that a relay of rooftop bonfires could spread word of a Saracen (Turkish pirate) attack. The gray-green trees are olives. Dark, green-leafed trees planted in dense groves are the source of the region's lemons—many destined to become *limoncello* liqueur. The black nets over the orange and lemon groves create a greenhouse effect, trapping warmth and humidity for maximum tastiness, while offering protection from hail and birds (preserving the peels used for *limoncello*).

Atop the ridge outside of Sorrento, look to your right: The two small islands after Sorrento are the **Galli Islands;** the bigger one, on the left, is Ulysses Island. These islands, once owned by the famed ballet dancer Rudolf Nureyev, mark the boundary between the Bay of Naples and the Bay of Salerno. Technically, the Amalfi Coast drive begins here.

The limestone cliffs that plunge into the sea were traversed by an ancient trail that became a modern road in the mid-19th century. Fruit stands sell produce from farms and orchards just over the hill. Limestone absorbs the heat, making this south-facing coastline a suntrap, with temperatures as much as 10 degrees higher than in nearby Sorrento. Bougainvillea and geraniums grow like weeds here in the summer.

As you approach the exotic-looking town of **Positano,** you know you've reached the scenic heart of the Amalfi Coast. Views of Positano, the main stop along the coast, are dramatic on either side of town. Just south of Positano, **St. Peter's Hotel** (Il San Pietro di Positano, camouflaged below the tiny St. Peter's church) is just about the most posh stop on the coast. Notice the elevator to the beach and dock. Bring your credit card.

Praiano is notable for its cathedral, with the characteristic majolica-tiled roof and dome—a reminder of this region's respected ceramics industry. Just past the tunnel stands another Saracen watchtower.

Marina di Praiano is a tiny and unique fishing hamlet wedged into a tight ravine with a couple of good restaurants and some small hotels.

The next Saracen tower guarded the harbor of the Amalfi navy until the fleet was destroyed in 1343 by a tsunami caused by an earthquake.

The most striking stretch of coastline ends at **Amalfi** and **Atrani**. As you leave Amalfi, look up to the left. The white house that clings to a cliff (Villa Rondinaia) was home for many years to the writer Gore Vidal. Atop the cliff is the town of **Ravello**. From here, the western half of the Amalfi Coast is mostly wild and unpopulated until you hit **Salerno**, with the striking Greek temples at **Paestum**.

Positano

According to legend, the Greek god Poseidon created Positano for Pasitea, a nymph he lusted after. History says the town was founded when ancient Greeks at Paestum decided to move out

of the swamp (to escape the malaria carried by its mosquitoes). Specializing in scenery and sand, Positano hangs halfway between Sorrento and Amalfi town on the most spectacular stretch of the coast.

The village, a ▲▲▲ sight from a distance, is a pleasant gathering of cafés and expensive stores, with a good but pebbly beach. Positano is famous for its fashions—90 percent of its shops are women's clothing boutiques.

The "skyline" looks like it did a century ago. Notice the town's characteristic Saracen-inspired rooftop domes. Filled with sand, these provide low-tech insulation—to help buildings stay cool in summer and warm in winter. It's been practically impossible to get a building permit in Positano for 25 years now, and landowners who want to renovate can't make external changes. The steep stairs are a way of life for the 4,000 hardy locals. Only one street in Positano allows motorized traffic; the rest are steep pedestrian lanes. Because hotels don't take large groups (bus access is too difficult), the town—unlike Sorrento—has been spared the ravages of big-bus tourism.

Consider seeing Positano as a day trip from Sorrento: Take the bus out and the afternoon ferry home, but be sure to check the boat schedules when you arrive—the last ferry often leaves before 18:00. Or spend the night to enjoy the magic of Positano. The town has a local flavor at night, when the grown-ups stroll and the kids play soccer on the church porch.

Orientation to Positano

Squished into a ravine, with narrow alleys that cascade down to the harbor, Positano requires you to stroll, whether you're going up or heading down. The center of town has no main square (unless you count the beach). There's little to do here but eat, window-shop, and enjoy the beach and views...hence the town's popularity.

Tourist Information

The TI is a half-block from the beach, in a small building at the bottom of the church steps (April-Sept Mon-Sat 8:30-19:30, Sun 8:30-14:30, Oct-March generally Mon-Sat 9:00-14:30, tel. 089-875-067, www.aziendaturismopositano.it).

Arrival in Positano

The main coast highway winds above the town. Regional SITA buses (blue or green-and-white) stop at two scheduled bus stops located at either end of town: Chiesa Nuova (at Bar Internazionale, nearer Sorrento, use only if you're staying at Brikette Hostel) and Sponda (nearer Amalfi town). Although roads from both stops lead downhill through the town to the beach, Sponda is closer and less steep; from this stop, it's a 20-minute stroll/shop/munch to the beach (and TI).

If you're catching the SITA bus back to Sorrento, be aware that it may leave from the Sponda stop five minutes before the printed departure. There's no room for the bus to wait, so in case the driver is early, you should be, too (€3.60, departures about hourly, daily 7:00-22:00, until 20:00 off-season). Buy tickets from the tobacco shop next to Bar Mulino Verde or just below the bus stop at the Total gas station (across from Hotel Marincanto).

If the walk up to the stop is too tough, take the dizzy little local red-and-white shuttle bus (marked *Interno Positano*), which constantly loops through Positano, connecting the lower town with the highway's two bus stops (2/hour, €1.10 at tobacco shop or €1.50 on board, catch it at convenient stop at the corner of Via

AMALFI COAST

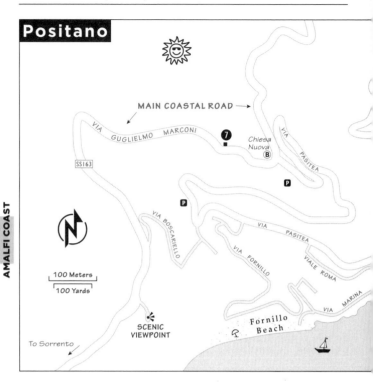

Positano

MAIN COASTAL ROAD →

VIA GUGLIELMO MARCONI

SS163

Chiesa Nuova

VIA PASITEA

VIA BOSCARIELLO

VIA PASITEA

VIA FORNILLO

VIALE ROMA

VIA MARINA

100 Meters
100 Yards

SCENIC VIEWPOINT

Fornillo Beach

To Sorrento

Colombo and Via dei Mulini, heads up to Sponda). Bar Mulino Verde, located off Piazza dei Mulini (as close as cars, taxis, and the shuttle bus can get to the beach), is just across from the shuttle bus stop, with a fine, breezy terrace you can enjoy if you're waiting.

Drivers must go with the one-way flow, entering the town only at the Chiesa Nuova bus stop (closest to Sorrento) and exiting at Sponda. Driving is a headache here. Parking is worse.

Helpful Hints

Internet Access: Your best bet is at **La Brezza Internet,** on the west side of the beach (to the right as you face the water).

Local Guide: Christine Ornelas, an Australian lawyer who fell for a local and married into the Positano scene, has become the town historian. She weaves her interests into a fascinating two-hour walk through town. Christine's tour gives the town context and brings meaning to fun hidden history, while offering an overview of the local scene, tastings of local products, and tips on shopping, beaches, restaurants, and excursions (€20, 2 people-€35 with this book, April-Oct Mon-Sat at 10:30, email or call to confirm—she'll do the tour for even just a couple of people, mobile 334-232-2096, www.discover

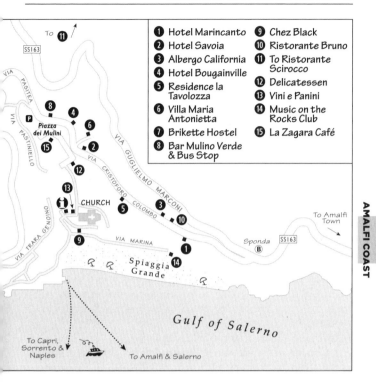

positano.it, christineornelas@gmail.com). Christine's walk starts at Piazza dei Mulini (outside the church, Chiesa del Rosario).

Self-Guided Walk

Welcome to Positano

While there's no real sightseeing in Positano, this short downhill guided stroll will help you get your bearings from top to bottom.

• *Start at...*

Piazza dei Mulini: This is the upper town meeting point—as close to the beach as vehicles can get—and is also the lower stop for the little red-and-white shuttle bus (2/hour, departs on the half-hour). Bar Mulino Verde is *the* local hangout—older people gather inside while the younger crowd congregates on the wisteria-draped terrace across the street. In this small town, gossiping is a big pastime.

Positano's ceramic and linen industries boomed when tourists discovered the place in the 1970s. The beach-inspired Moda Positano fashion label was first created as a break from the rigid dress code of the '50s. On this piazza, and throughout town, you'll find lots of ceramic and linen shops (and an abundance of ATMs), along with galleries featuring the work of local artists.

• *Wander downhill to the stepped fork in the road. You've reached...*

Midtown: At Enoteca Cuomo (#3), butcher Vincenzo stocks fine local red wines and is happy to explain their virtues. He also makes homemade sausages, salami, and *panini*—good for a quick lunch. The small set of stairs leads to the wonderful, recommended Delicatessen, where Emilia can fix you a good picnic. Their down-stairs café (past the stairs, on the left at #13) sells an array of tempting edible souvenirs.

La Zagara (across the lane at #10) is a pastry shop by day and a piano bar by night. Tempting pastries such as the rum-drenched *babà* (a local favorite) fill the window display. After-hours, it's filled with traditional Neapolitan music and dancing. A bit farther downhill, Brunella (#24) is respected for traditional, quality, and locally made linens.

Across the street, Hotel Palazzo Murat fills what was a grand Benedictine monastery. Step into the plush courtyard to enjoy the scene. Continuing on, under a fragrant bougainvillea trellis, you'll come to "street merchants' gulch," where artisans display their goodies.

• *Continue to Piazza Flavio Gioia, with the big...*

Church of Santa Maria Assunta: This church originated as the abbey of Positano's 12th-century Benedictine monastery. Originally Romanesque, it was eventually abandoned (along with the entire lower town) out of fear of pirate attacks. When the coast was clear in the 18th century, the church was given an extreme Baroque makeover. Its dome is covered in colorful majolica tiles.

Inside (first chapel on left) is a fine manger scene *(presepe)*. Its original 18th-century figurines give you an idea of the folk cos-tumes of the age. The Black Madonna, an icon-like Byzantine painting (above the altar), was likely brought here in the 12th cen-tury by Benedictine monks. But locals prefer the romantic legend: Saracen pirates had it on their ship as plunder. A violent storm hit—sure to sink the evil ship. The painting of Mary spoke, saying, *"Posa posa"* (lay me down), and the ship glided safely to this harbor. The pirates were so stricken they became Christians. Locals kept the painting, and the town became known as *Posa-tano* (recalling Mary's command). To the right of the altar, a small chapel holds a silver and copper bust of St. Vitus—the town patron who brought Christianity here in about A.D. 300. In the adjacent niche is a rare painting of baby Jesus being circumcised (by Fabrizio Santafede, 1599), considered the finest historic painting in town.

Back outside, you'll see the bell tower, dating from 1707. Above the door, it sports a Romanesque relief scavenged from the original church. The scene—a wolf mermaid with seven little fish—was a reminder to worshippers of how integral the sea was to their livelihood.

• *Backtrack up the steps, circling the church around to the left.*

Around the Church: Around the side of the church, find the plaque describing in English how this spot once held a Roman villa, buried when Mount Vesuvius erupted in A.D. 79. Only a few minor rooms have been excavated (a photograph shows one of the preserved frescoes). The rest await discovery—digging has ceased until there are enough funds to do it properly. The stairs lead down to a glass door that offers a peek into the church's crypt—originally the early church's altar. According to local legend, the Benedictines sat their dead brothers on the stone choir chairs here to decompose and remind all of their mortality.

• *Continue climbing down the steps arcing to the right. You'll eventually come to the little square facing the beach.*

Piazzetta: This is the local gathering point in the evening, as local boys hustle tourist girls into the nearby nightclub. Residents traded their historic baptistery font with Amalfi town for the two iron lions you see facing the beach. From here, you can look up and admire the colorful majolica tiles so typical of church domes in this region. Positano was once a notable naval power, with many shipyards along this beach. These eventually became fishermen's quarters and storehouses, and later, today's tourist restaurants. The Positano **beach,** called Spiaggia Grande, is half public (no shower) and half private.

• *On the far left side of the beach is...*

Music on the Rocks: This chic, recommended club is all that's left of the 1970s scene when Positano really rocked. While it's dead until about 23:00, you're welcome to wander into the cool troglodisco interior for a drink.

• *Wander across the beach. Beyond the kiosks that sell boat tickets, a path climbs up and over, past a 13th-century lookout fort from Saracen pirate days, to the next beach. It's a worthwhile little five-minute walk to...*

Fornillo Beach: This is where locals go for better swimming and to escape some of the tourist crowds.

• *Our walk is over. Time to relax.*

Sights in Positano

Beaches—Positano's pebbly and sandy primary beach, **Spiaggia Grande,** is colorful with umbrellas as it stretches wide around the cove. It's mostly private (€10-15/person, April-Oct, cost includes drink service and use of lounge chair and umbrella), with a free section near the middle, close to where the boats take off. The nearest WC is beneath the steps to the right (as you face the water).

Fornillo Beach, a less-crowded option just around the bend (to the west) of Spiaggia Grande, is favored by residents, with more affordable chair and umbrella rentals. This beach is lined by humble snack bars and lunch eateries.

Boat Trips—At the west end of Spiaggia Grande (to the right as you face the sea), booths sell at tickets to a number of destinations. Consider renting a rowboat or taking a boat tour to a nearby cave (La Grotta dello Smeraldo—Emerald Cave), fishing village (Nerano), or small islands.

Ferries run to Amalfi, Capri, and Sorrento.

Shopping—Locally produced linens and ceramics can be found at shops and galleries throughout town. **Ceramica Assunta,** one of the oldest ceramics stores in Positano, carries colorful Solimene dinnerware and more at two locations (Via Colombo 97 and Via Colombo 137, tel. 089-875-008). The young owner-artisan couple at **Sunflower Bottega d'Arte** make and paint their own ceramic designs. Two popular (and pricey) fashion boutiques are **Brunella** (Via Pasitea 72, tel. 089-875-228) and **Pepito's** (Via Pasitea 39, tel. 089-875-446).

Nightlife—The big-time action in the old town center is the impressive club **Music on the Rocks,** literally carved into the rocks on the beach (opens at 22:00 mid-April-Oct but party starts about 23:30, €10-20 cover charge includes a drink, go to dance or just check out the scene, Via Grotte Dell'Incanto 51, tel. 089-875-874, www.musicontherocks.it). For a more low-key atmosphere, café/pastry shop **La Zagara** hosts music nightly in summer (June-Sept, starts around 21:00, Via dei Mulini 10, tel. 089-875-964).

Sleeping in Positano

These hotels (but not the hostel) are all on Via Colombo, which leads from the SITA Sponda bus stop down into the village. Prices given are for the highest season (June-Sept)—at other times, they become soft. Most places close in the winter (Dec-Feb or longer). Expect to pay more than €20 a day to park.

$$$ Hotel Marincanto is a newly restored four-star hotel with a bright breakfast terrace practically teetering on a cliff. Suites seem to be designed for a *luna di miele*—honeymoon (Db-€210 mid-April-mid-Oct, €170 off-season, more expensive superior rooms and suites, elevator, Wi-Fi, pool, private stairs to beach, parking-€24/day, closed Nov-March, 50 yards below Sponda bus stop at Via Colombo 50, tel. 089-875-130, fax 089-875-595, www .marincanto.it, info@marincanto.it).

$$ Hotel Savoia is family-run, with 39 sizeable, breezy, bright air-conditioned rooms (viewless Db-€130, view Db-€180, deluxe Db-€200, at least €10/day off with this book in 2012, eleva-

---

Sleep Code

(€1 = about $1.40, country code: 39)
S = Single, **D** = Double/Twin, **T** = Triple, **Q** = Quad, **b** = bathroom,
s = shower only. Unless otherwise noted, credit cards are
accepted, English is spoken, and breakfast is included.

To help you sort easily through these listings, I've divided
the accommodations into three categories based on the price
for a standard double room with bath:

$$$ Higher Priced—Most rooms €180 or more.
$$ Moderately Priced—Most rooms between €120-180.
$ Lower Priced—Most rooms €120 or less.

Prices can change without notice; verify the hotel's
current rates online or by email. For other updates, see www
.ricksteves.com/update.

AMALFI COAST

---

tor, Wi-Fi, closed Nov-Feb, Via Colombo 73, tel. 089-875-003,
fax 089-811-844, www.savoiapositano.it, info@savoiapositano.it,
Regina and daughters Mechy, Piera, and Cristina).

$$ Albergo California has lofty views, 15 spacious rooms,
and a grand terrace draped with vines. The Cinque family—Maria,
John, and Antonio—will welcome you (view Db-€160 June-Sept,
€10 less April-May and Oct, prices promised with this book
through 2012, air-con, Wi-Fi, free parking, closed Dec-March,
Via Colombo 141, tel. 089-875-382, fax 089-812-154, www.hotel
californiapositano.it, info@hotelcaliforniapositano.it).

$$ Hotel Bougainville rents 16 comfortable rooms, half
with balconies. Everything's bright, modern, and tasteful (view-
less Db-€119-140, view Db-€175, 5 percent off these rates with
this book in 2012, check website for specials, air-con, closed Nov-
March, Via Colombo 25, tel. 089-875-047, www.bougainville.it,
info@bougainville.it, friendly Marella).

$ Residence la Tavolozza is an attractive eight-room hotel,
warmly run by Celeste (cheh-LEHS-tay) and daughters Francesca
and Paola. Each cheerily tiled room comes with a view, a terrace,
and silence. This is a good value (Db-€90-120 depending on size,
these prices promised through 2012 with this book, families can
ask for "Royal Apartment," cash only, call to confirm if arriving
late, lavish breakfast extra, air-con, closed Dec-Feb, Via Colombo
10, tel. & fax 089-875-040, www.latavolozzapositano.it, celeste
.dileva@tiscali.it).

$ Villa Maria Antonietta is a humble, no-frills place with
seven backpacker rooms, all with a distant view of the sea. Head
down a grungy lane off the elegant main drag and then up a few

big flights of stairs (Db-€120, often cheaper, follow signs from Via Colombo 69, tel. 089-875-071, www.villamariaantonietta.com, Maria).

$ Brikette Hostel offers your best cheap dorm-bed option in this otherwise ritzy town. Renting 25 beds and offering a great sun and breakfast terrace, it's bright and clean with the normal hostel rules: 11:00-14:30 lockout and cushy curfew at 2:00 in the morning for dorm rooms, and no membership required. Friendly Cristiana is full of energy, organizes parties several times a week, and offers discounted prices for excursions (bed in 4- to 8-bed dorms-€23, D-€65, Db-€75, bigger family rooms, these prices with cash; hearty breakfast extra but cheap, €5 dinners; free Wi-Fi, may be closed Dec-Feb, leave bus at Chiesa Nuova/Bar Internazionale stop and backtrack uphill 500 feet to Via G. Marconi 358, tel. & fax 089-875-857, www.brikette.com, info@brikette.com).

Eating in Positano

Waterfront Dining: The pizzerias and restaurants facing the beach, while overpriced, are pleasant and convenient. At the waterfront, I like **Chez Black,** which is known for its seafood (down the steps, to the right), but neighboring places also leave people fat and happy.

"Uptown": The unassuming, family-run **Ristorante Bruno** is handy if you don't want to hike down into the town center for dinner (near the top of Via Colombo at #157).

"Way Uptown": **Ristorante Scirocco** is a worthy splurge, perched high above Positano with fantastic views and equally fine meals ranging from seafood to steak. Get there with enough daylight left to enjoy the scenery (€12 *primi*, €18 *secondi*, €35 fixed-price meal, daily 12:00-15:00 & 19:00-24:00, closed Nov-Easter, call to arrange a free shuttle, Via Montepertuso 126, tel. 089-875-184).

Picnics: If a picnic dinner on your balcony or the beach sounds good, sunny Emilia at **Delicatessen** can supply the ingredients (*antipasto misto* to go at €1.40/100 grams, pasta for €1/100 grams, sandwiches made and sold by weight—about €3.50, she microwaves food and includes all the picnic ware, come early for best selection; daily March-Oct 7:00-22:00, Nov-Feb 8:00-20:00, just below car park at Via del Mulini 5, tel. 089-875-489). **Vini e Panini,** another small grocery, is a block from the beach a few steps above the TI. Daniela, the fifth-generation owner, speaks English and happily makes sandwiches to order. Choose from the "Caprese" (mozzarella and tomato), the "Positano" (mozzarella, tomato, and ham), or create your own (priced by weight, around €3.50 each). They also have a nice selection of well-priced regional wines (daily 8:00-22:00, off-season closes 14:00-16:00, just off church steps, tel. 089-875-175).

Positano Connections

Always check boat schedules, since the last boats often leave Positano before 18:00. The schedule varies drastically according to time of year; it's more reliable in summer than off-season, but be sure to check it with the TI. There's no real dock, so stormy weather can disrupt schedules. If you're thinking of taking a Capri trip from Positano, consider a boat that goes directly to the Blue Grotto (rather than dropping you in the port to catch another boat from there).

From Positano by Boat to: Amalfi (6/day, 30 minutes, €7), **Capri** (mid-April-mid-Oct, 2-4/day, 35-50 minutes, €15-17; less off-season), **Sorrento** (mid-April-mid-Oct only, 2-4/day, 40 minutes, €11), **Salerno** (mid-April-Sept only, 4-6/day, 70 minutes, €11). Check schedules carefully as most boats run only mid-April to mid-October; few run off-season. Direct boats to **Naples** run several times a day in the summer (check with the TI); you can also change boats in Sorrento or Capri.

Near Positano: Marina di Praiano

Wedged into a tight ravine between Positano and Amalfi town, this tiny fishing hamlet has a pint-sized beach (half free, half pay), a couple of restaurants, and a few small hotels. All Sorrento-Positano buses stop at the top of the village. Parking is pricey (blue spots-€3/hour, pay and display). If you're staying here overnight, hotels can arrange a cheaper spot.

Sleeping in Marina di Praiano: Consider **$ La Conchiglia da Antonio,** a bar that rents 12 rooms across the ravine (Db-€60, €80 in July, €100 in Aug, extra bed-€20, mention this book when reserving; includes small breakfast, tel. 089-874-313, www.la conchigliapraiano.it, info@laconchigliapraiano.it). **$$ Hotel Alfonso a Mare** rents 15 rooms (Db-€120, €200 in Aug when it includes obligatory dinner, tel. 089-874-091, www.alfonsoamare .it, info@alfonsoamare.it).

Amalfi Town

The Amalfi Coast is named for this town. It was founded (according to legend) when the girlfriend of Hercules was buried here. After Rome fell, Amalfi was one of the first cities to trade goods—coffee, carpets, and paper—between Europe and points east. Its heyday was the 10th and 11th centuries, when it was a powerful maritime republic—a trading power with a fleet that controlled this region and rivaled Genoa and Venice.

The Republic of Amalfi founded a hospital in Jerusalem and claims to have founded the Knights of Malta order—even giving them the Amalfi cross, which became the famous Maltese cross. Amalfi minted its own coins and established "rules of the sea"—the basics of which survive today. Paper has been a vital industry here since the glory days in the Middle Ages. They'd pound rags into pulp in a big vat, pull it up using a screen, and air-dry it to create paper (the same technique used to make paper still sold in Amalfi shops). For a demonstration of this ancient technique, check out the Paper Museum (see "Sights in Amalfi Town," later).

In 1343, this little powerhouse was suddenly destroyed by a tsunami caused by an undersea earthquake. That disaster, compounded by devastating plagues, left Amalfi a humble backwater. Today, its 7,000 residents live off tourism (and paper). Amalfi is not as picturesque as Positano or as well-connected as Sorrento, but take some time to explore the town. Amalfi's charms will reveal themselves, especially early and late in the day, when the tourist crowds dissipate.

Orientation to Amalfi Town

The waterfront of this town is dominated by a bus station, a parking lot, two gas stations, a statue of local boy Flavio Gioia—the purported inventor of the compass (see sidebar)—and a TI.

Amalfi, the most big-bus accessible of the towns along the coast, is a classic tourist trap. It's packed during the day with big-bus tours (whose drivers pay €50 an hour to park while their groups shop for *limoncello* and ceramics).

Before you enter the town, notice the colorful tile above the Porta della Marina gateway, showing off the domain of the maritime Republic of Amalfi. Just to the left, along the busy road, are a series of arches that indicate the long, narrow, vaulted halls of its

> # Flavio Gioia
>
> You'll see a statue of Flavio Gioia towering above the chaos of cars and buses on the seaside piazza. Amalfi residents credit this hometown boy with the invention of the magnetic compass back in 1302, but historians can't verify that he actually existed. While an improvement to the compass did occur in Amalfi during that time period, the Chinese and Arabs had been using rudimentary compasses for years. In Gioia's time, seamen placed a magnetized needle on the surface of a container of water as a kind of medieval GPS. If Gioia existed at all, he probably just figured out how to secure that needle inside a little box. Locals, however, have no doubts that Flavio Gioia was an inventor extraordinaire.

arsenal—where ships were built in the 11th century.

Venture into the town, and you find its once rich and formidable medieval shell is filled with trendy shops, a main square sporting a springwater-spewing statue of St. Andrew, and a cathedral—the town's most important sight.

The farther you get away from the water, the more traditional Amalfi gets. The Paper Museum is a 10-minute walk up Via Lorenzo d'Amalfi, the main drag. From here, the road narrows and you can turn off onto a path leading to the shaded Valle dei Mulini; it's full of paper-mill ruins that recall this once proud and prosperous industry. The ruined castle clinging to the rocky ridge above Amalfi is Torre dello Ziro, a good lookout point for intrepid hikers.

Tourist Information

The TI is about 100 yards south of the center, next to the post office; facing the sea, it's to the left (generally Mon-Fri 9:00-13:00 & 14:00-18:00, Sat 9:00-13:00, closed Sun, shorter hours off-season, Corso della Repubbliche Marinare 27, tel. 089-871-107, www.amalfitouristoffice.it, info@amalfitouristoffice.it).

Helpful Hints

Don't Get Stranded: Be warned—the last bus back to Sorrento leaves at 20:00 (at 22:00 June-Sept) and can be full. Without a public bus, your only option is a €100 taxi ride.

Internet Access: The travel agency **L'Altra Costiera,** on the main drag a block up from the church, has several terminals with Internet access (daily 9:00-21:00, Via Lorenzo d'Amalfi 34, tel. 089-873-6082).

Hiking Guidebook: The best book on hiking is *Sorrento Amalfi Capri Car Tours and Walks,* on sale at many local bookstores. It has useful color-coded maps and info on public transportation to the trailheads.

Baggage Storage: You can store your bag safely for €3 at the **Divina Costiera Travel Office** facing the waterfront square, across from the bus parking area (daily 8:00-13:00 & 14:00-19:30, tel. 089-872-467).

Laundry: The full-service **Lavalampo** offers same-day service (€5/kilo—2.2 pounds—wash and dry, Mon-Sat 8:30-13:00 & 16:30-20:00, closed Thu afternoon and Sun; drop off before 9:30 and pick up same day). It's a four-minute walk up the main drag (#51) from the cathedral.

Speedboat Charters: To hire your own boat for a tour of the coastline from Amalfi (or to Capri), consider **Charter La Dolce Vita** (mobile 335-549-9365, www.amalficoastyacht.it).

Sights in Amalfi Town

Cathedral—This church is "Amalfi Romanesque" (a mix of Moorish and Byzantine flavors, built c. 1000-1300) with a fanciful Neo-Byzantine facade from the 19th century. Climb the imposing stairway—which functions as a handy outdoor theater for town events. The 1,000-year-old bronze door at the top was given to Amalfi by a wealthy local merchant who had it made in Constantinople.

Cost and Hours: €3, daily 7:30-19:30, shorter hours off-season, closed Jan-Feb, from 10:00-17:00 access church through cloister, tel. 089-871-324. There's a fine, free WC at the top of the steps (through unmarked green door, just a few steps before ticket booth, ask for key at desk).

Touring the Cathedral: Pick up the English flier as you enter. Visitors are directed on a one-way circuit through the cathedral complex with four stops.

This courtyard of 120 graceful columns—the **"Cloister of Paradise"**—was the cemetery for local nobles in the 13th century (note their stone sarcophagi). Don't miss the fine view of the bell tower and its majolica tiles.

The original ninth-century church, known as the **Basilica of the Crucifix,** is now a museum filled with the art treasures of the cathedral. The Angevin Mitre (Mitra Angioina), with a "pavement of tiny pearls" setting off its gold and gems, has been worn by bishops since the 14th century. On the far wall is a plank from a Saracen pirate ship that wrecked just outside of town in 1544 during a freak storm. Believers credit St. Andrew with causing the storm that saved the town from certain Turkish pillage and plunder.

Just as Venice needed Mark to get on the pilgrimage map, Amalfi needed St. Andrew—one of the apostles who, along with his brother (St. Peter), left their fishing nets to become the original "fishers of men." What are believed to be his remains (in the **Crypt of St. Andrew,** under the huge bronze statue) were brought here from Constantinople in 1206 during the Crusades—an indication of the wealth and importance of Amalfi back then.

The **cathedral** interior is notable for its fine 13th-century wooden crucifix. The painting behind it shows St. Andrew martyred on an X-shaped cross flanked by two Egyptian granite columns supporting a triumphal arch. Before leaving, check out the delicate mother-of-pearl crucifix (right of door in back).

▲**Paper Museum**—At this cavernous, cool 13th-century paper mill-turned-museum, a multilingual guide collects groups at the entrance (no particular times) for a 25-minute tour that recounts the history and process of papermaking, a long-time industry for the town of Amalfi (€4, March-Oct daily 10:00-18:30, sporadic hours Nov-Feb; a 10-minute walk up the main street from the cathedral, look for signs to *Museo della Carta;* tel. 089-830-4561, www.museodellacarta.it).

Hikes

Amalfi is the starting point for several fine hikes. Here are two:

Hike #1—This loop trail leads up the valley past paper-mill ruins, ending in the tiny town of **Pontone;** you can get lunch there, and head back down to the town of Amalfi (allow 3 hours total). Bring a good map, since it's easy to veer off the main route. Start your hike by following the main road (Via Lorenzo d'Amalfi) away from the sea.

After the Paper Museum, jog right, then left to join the trail, which runs through the shaded woods along a babbling stream. Heed the signs that warn people to stay away from the ruins of paper mills (no matter how tempting), since many are ready to collapse on unwary hikers. Continue up to Pontone, where Trattoria l'Antico Borgo offers wonderful cuisine and a great view (Via Noce 4, tel. 089-871-469). After lunch, return to Amalfi via a steep stairway.

If you're feeling ambitious, before you head back to Amalfi, add a one-hour detour (30 minutes each way) to visit the ridge-hugging **Torre dello Ziro** (ask a local how to find the trail to this tower). You'll be rewarded with a spectacular view.

Hike #2—For an easier hike (more of a walk), head to the nearby town of **Atrani.** This village, just a 15-minute stroll beyond Amalfi town, is a world apart; its 1,500 residents consider themselves definitely *not* from Amalfi. Leave Amalfi via the main road, and stay on the water side until the sidewalk ends. Cross the street and head up the stairs; the paved route takes you over the hill, and drops you into Atrani in about 15 minutes. Piazza Umberto is the core of town, with cafés and a little grocery store that makes sandwiches. Amazingly, Atrani has none of the trendy resort feel of Amalfi, with relatively few tourists, a delightful town square, and a free, sandy beach (if you drive here, pay for parking at harbor). This town also has some recommended accommodations.

From Atrani, you can continue up to **Ravello.** But be warned: Unless you're part mountain goat, you'll probably prefer catching the bus to Ravello from Amalfi town instead.

Sleeping in Amalfi Town

(€1 = about $1.40, country code: 39)

Sleeps are better in Positano, but if you're marooned in Amalfi, here are some options. High season on the Amalfi Coast (especially July-Sept) demands the highest prices; prices listed here are peak-season rates (roughly April-Oct).

$$ Hotel La Bussola, a five-minute walk north along the harbor, rises above the ocean with 60 sunny rooms, most boasting terraces with a breezy ocean view (Sb-€90, Db-€140, Signor Dilieto offers a 10 percent Rick Steves discount in 2012 when you book direct, air-con, Wi-Fi, parking-€15/day, Lungomare dei Cavalieri 16, tel. 089-871-533, www.labussolahotel.it, info@la bussolahotel.it).

$$ Hotel Amalfi, with 40 rooms and a garden, lacks warmth but is an acceptable choice (Db-€80-120, peaks at €160 Aug-Sept, €10 cash discount, air-con, Wi-Fi, roof-terrace breakfast, no sea views; 50 yards from cathedral—head up the pedestrian street and take staircase to the left before underpass, Via dei Pastai 3; tel. 089-872-440, fax 089-872-250, www.hamalfi.it, info@hamalfi.it).

$ Residenza del Duca is a fancy little seven-room boutique B&B taking advantage of its wonderful location in the heart of this touristy enclave (minuscule Sb-€60, Db-€90, €130 Aug-Sept, €10 discount with this book and cash, air-con, Wi-Fi, glimpses of ocean through the rooftops; 25 yards uphill from Piazza Duomo, take the first left, go up the stairs and follow the signs, then go up more stairs—over 70 total—to Via Mastalo II Duca 3; call for luggage service, tel. 089-873-6365, www.residencedelduca.it, info @residencedelduca.it, Andrea).

Nearby in Atrani

Accommodation options are limited in Atrani, a small-town Amalfi hideaway without the glitz and hill-climbing of Positano (described under "Hike #2," earlier).

$ A'Scalinatella is a dingy, informal backpackers' hostel, with a honeycomb of cramped 3- to 10-bed dorms, way-over-priced private rooms, and a communal kitchen (dorm bed-€25, D-€60, Db-€90, prices very soft, cash only, no hostel membership required, 100 yards up from main square at #5 on Scalinatella Piazza Umberto I, tel. 089-871-492, www.hostelscalinatella.com, info@hostelscalinatella.com). It's run by English-speaking owners Filippo and Gabriele, who also rent rooms scattered all over town.

$ L'Argine Fiorito B&B, which stands like a little castle overlooking a ravine at the top of town, rents five tidy and tiled rooms (Db-€100, extra bed-€35, tel. 089-873-6309, mobile 347-531-1158, www.larginefiorito.it, info@larginefiorito.it).

Ravello

Ravello sits atop a lofty perch 1,000 feet above the sea and offers an interesting church, two villas, and a chance to catch a glimpse of celebrities. American author Gore Vidal, who lived here for decades, is one of a sizable group of rich and famous artists—including Richard Wagner, D. H. Lawrence, Henry Wadsworth Longfellow, and Greta Garbo—who have succumbed to Ravello's charms.

To see the sights listed here, start at the bus stop and walk through the tunnel to the main square, where you'll find the church on the right, Villa Rufolo on the left, and the **TI** (daily May-Oct 9:00-19:00, Nov-April 9:00-17:00, 100 yards from the square—follow signs to Via Roma 18, tel. 089-857-096, www.ravellotime.com). A 10-minute walk through the town (follow the signs) leads to Villa Cimbrone.

Sights in Ravello

Duomo—You can't miss Ravello's cathedral, located right on the main square. The main features of this church are the bronze doors, with 54 scenes of the life of Christ, the carved marble pulpit supported by six lions, and a chance to climb behind the altar for a close-up look at the relic of holy blood. The geometric designs show Arabic influence. The humble cathedral museum is two rooms of well-described carved marble that evoke the historical importance of the town.

Cost and Hours: Church—free, daily May-Oct 9:00-12:30 & 17:00-20:00, closes earlier off-season; museum—€2, daily 9:00-19:00; you can generally get into the church all day long via the museum, entrance on the right, tel. 089-858-311.

Villa Rufolo—The villa, built in the 13th century, is only a barren ruin today. It has pleasant Arabic/Norman gardens, which provide a delightful frame for the commanding coastline view (you can enjoy the same view, without the entry fee, from the bus parking lot just below the villa). It's also one of the venues for Ravello's annual arts festival, which runs from July through September (www.ravellofestival.com). During the concert season (April-Oct), concertgoers perch on a bandstand on the edge of the cliff for a combination of wonderful music and dizzying views. Wagner visited here and was impressed enough to set the second act of his opera *Parsifal* in the villa's magical gardens. A concert on the cliff is a sublime experience.

Cost and Hours: Villa entry-€5, daily May-Sept 9:00-20:00, Oct-April 9:00 until sunset, may close earlier if hosting a concert, tel. 089-857-621, concert information tel. 089-858-149, www.ravelloarts.org.

Villa Cimbrone—This villa, located at the other end of Ravello, was built in the 20th century by Englishman William Beckett. It offers extensive gardens and a killer view from the "Terrace of Infinity." Consider buying a picnic in town and discreetly munching it here, with magnificent Italian panoramas at your feet. A wander through the gardens will reveal reproductions of famous sculptures and lots of great views.

Cost and Hours: €6, daily 9:00-19:00, last entry 45 minutes before closing, tel. 089-857-459.

▲**Hike to Amalfi Town from Villa Cimbrone**—To walk downhill from Ravello's Villa Cimbrone to the town of Amalfi (a path for hardy hikers only—follow the TI's map), retrace your steps back toward town. Take the first left, which turns into a stepped path winding its way below the cliff. Pause here to look back up at the rock with a big white mansion—Villa La Rondinaia, where Gore Vidal lived for many years. Continue down the fairly steep path about 40 minutes to the town of Atrani, where several bars on the main square offer well-deserved refreshment. From here, it's about a 15-minute walk back to Amalfi.

Eating & Sleeping in Ravello

Ristorante Garden clings to the hillside and serves up unbeatable views of the coastline below—along with delicious homemade pasta. Savor a relaxing lunch on their terrace. Make sure to save room for the local favorite, *delizia al limone*—calling it a "lemon cream puff" doesn't begin to do it justice (€13 pastas, €16 *secondi*, daily 12:00-15:00 & 19:30-22:00, closed Tue off-season and Jan, next to Villa Rufolo—facing the church walk to the right through the tunnel to Via Boccaccio 4, tel. 089-857-226). They also rent nine basic but comfortable rooms, all with balconies and the same sweeping views (Db-€120-140, air-con, Wi-Fi, www.garden ravello.com, info@gardenravello.com, Anna).

Ravello Connections

Ravello and the town of Amalfi are connected by a winding road and a bus. Coming from Amalfi town, buy your ticket at the bar on the waterfront, and ask where the bus stop is (buses usually stop to the left as you face the water, near the statue on the waterfront by Piazza Flavio Gioia). In Ravello, line up early, since the buses are often crowded (2/hour, 25 minutes, €2.40, buy ticket in tobacco shop; catch bus 100 yards off main square, just past tunnel).

AMALFI COAST

Paestum

Paestum (PASTE-oom) has one of the best collections of Greek temples anywhere—and certainly the most accessible to Western

Europe. Serenely situated, Paestum is surrounded by fields and wildflowers, and has a sandy beach and only a modest commercial strip.

This town was founded as Poseidonia by Greeks in the sixth century B.C., and became a key stop on an important trade route. In the fifth century B.C., the Lucanians, a barbarous inland tribe, conquered Poseidonia, changed its name to Paistom, and tried to adopt the cultured ways of the Greeks. The Romans, who took over in the third century B.C., gave Paestum the name it bears today. The final conquerors of Paestum, malaria-carrying mosquitoes, kept the site wonderfully deserted for nearly a thousand years. Rediscovered in the 18th century, Paestum today offers the only well-preserved Greek ruins north of Sicily.

Planning Your Time

Allow two hours, including the museum. Depending on your interest and the heat, start with either the site or the museum. You'll enjoy the best light and smallest crowds late in the day.

Orientation to Paestum

Tourist Information: At the TI, next to the Paestum Archaeological Museum, pick up a free info booklet of the site (TI open daily 9:00-16:00, tel. 082-881-1016, www.infopaestum.it, info @infopaestum.it).

Arrival at Paestum: Buses from Salerno (see "Paestum Connections," at the end of this chapter) stop near a corner of the ruins (at a little bar/café). Or, if you're arriving by train, exit the station and walk through the old city gate; the ruins are an eight-minute walk straight ahead.

Cost: €4 for the museum, €4 for the site, €6.50 combo-ticket covers both.

Hours: Both museum and site open daily at 9:00 (except the first and third Mon of each month, when the museum is closed). Year-round, the museum closes at 19:30 (last ticket sold at 18:45). The site closes one hour before sunset (as late as 19:30 June-July, as early as 15:30 in winter, last site ticket sold one hour before closing, tel. 082-881-1023).

Information: There's little English information at the site itself. Several mediocre guidebooks are offered at the museum's bookshop, including a €15 past-and-present guide. Dull €5 audioguides are available to rent at the site entrance and cover both museum and site (ID required). Or you can follow my self-guided tours, below.

Local Guide: Silvia Braggio is a good guide who gives a fine two-hour walk of the site and museum (special rate with this book-€100, mobile 347-643-2307, www.silviaguide.it, silvia@silvia guide.it).

Eating: A couple of typical, touristy eateries flank the TI and site entrance. Your best lunch option is **Ristorante Nettuno** (quality food, reasonable prices, great setting, good temple views from tables, located at south entrance).

Entry: The site and museum have separate entrances. The museum, just outside the ruins, is in a cluster with the TI and a small paleo-Christian basilica.

Self-Guided Tours

Paestum Archaeological Site

This tour begins at the Temple of Ceres, goes through the center of the Roman town past the Greek Memorial Tomb, circles around the other two Greek temples, then leaves the site to walk down the modern road to the Ekklesiasterion (which faces the museum). With this information, most visitors will not need to rent the audioguide or buy a book.

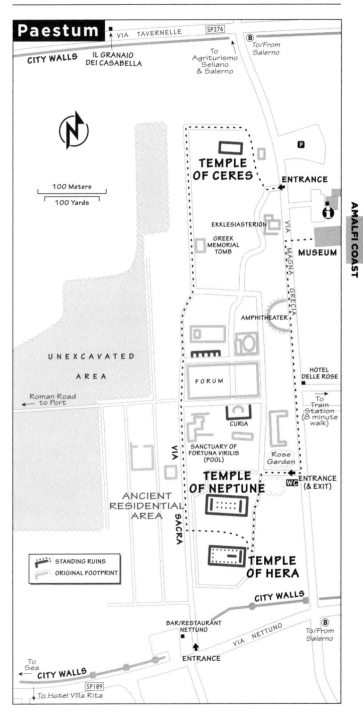

Paestum

VIA TAVERNELLE   SP276

To/From Salerno B

CITY WALLS   IL GRANAIO DEI CASABELLA

To Agriturismo Seliano & Salerno

N

100 Meters

100 Yards

TEMPLE OF CERES

P

ENTRANCE

EKKLESIASTERION

GREEK MEMORIAL TOMB

i

VIA MAGNA GRECIA

MUSEUM

UNEXCAVATED AREA

AMPHITHEATER

Roman Road to Port

HOTEL DELLE ROSE

To Train Station (8 minute walk)

FORUM

CURIA

SANCTUARY OF FORTUNA VIRILIS (POOL)

Rose Garden

TEMPLE OF NEPTUNE   WC   ENTRANCE (& EXIT)

ANCIENT RESIDENTIAL AREA

VIA SACRA

TEMPLE OF HERA

STANDING RUINS

ORIGINAL FOOTPRINT

CITY WALLS

BAR/RESTAURANT NETTUNO

VIA NETTUNO   B   To/From Salerno

ENTRANCE

To Sea   CITY WALLS

SP189

To Hotel Villa Rita

Background: While Paestum is famous for its marvelous Greek temples, much of what you see is Roman. Five elements of Greek Paestum survive: three misnamed temples, a memorial tomb, and a circular meeting place (or Ekklesiasterion). The rest, including the wall that defines the site, is Roman.

Paestum was once a seaport (the ocean is now about a mile away—the wall in the distance, which stretches about three miles, is about halfway to today's coastline). Only about a fifth of the site has been excavated. The Greek city, which archaeologists figure had a population of about 13,000, was first conquered by Lucanians (who were pretty crude and made almost no changes in the physical city), and then by the Romans (who completely made it over).

The remaining Greek structures survive because the Romans were superstitious—they respected sacred areas, and didn't mess with temples and tombs. While most old Christian churches are built upon Roman temples (it's just what people do when they conquer another culture), no Roman temple is built upon a Greek temple. Romans appreciated how religion could function as the opiate of the masses. As long as people paid their taxes and obeyed the emperor's dictates, the practical Romans had no problem with any religion. The three Greek temples that you'll see here today have stood for about 2,500 years.

• *Buy your ticket, enter the site, and stand in front of the...*

Temple of Ceres: All three Paestum temples have inaccurate names, coined by 19th-century archaeologists who based their "discoveries" on wishful thinking. (While the Romans made things easy by leaving lots of inscriptions, the Greeks did not.) Those 1800s archaeologists wanted this temple to be devoted to Ceres, the goddess of agriculture. However, all the little votive statues found later,

when modern archaeologists dug here, instead depicted a woman with a big helmet: Athena, goddess of wisdom and war. (The Greeks' female war goddess was also the goddess of wisdom—thinking...strategy...female. The Romans' masculine war god was Mars—just fighting.) Each temple is part of a sanctuary—an open, sacred space around the temple. Because regular people couldn't go into the temple, the altar logically stood outside.

The Temple of Ceres dates from 500 B.C. It's made of locally quarried limestone blocks. Good roads and shipping didn't come along until the Romans, so the Greeks' buildings were limited to local materials. The wooden roof is long gone. Like the other two temples, this one was once painted white, black, and red, and has an east-west orientation—facing the rising sun. This temple's *cella* (interior room) is gone, cleared out when it was used as a Christian church in the sixth century. In medieval times, Normans scavenged stones from here; chunks of these temples can be found in Amalfi's cathedral.

Walk around to the back side of the Temple of Ceres. The capitals broke in a modern earthquake, so a steel bar provides necessary support. Each of the Paestum temples is Doric style—with three stairs, columns without a base, and shafts that narrow at the top to a simple capital of a round then a square block. While there were no carved reliefs, colorful frescoes once decorated the pediments.

As you walk away, look back at the temple. Traditionally, Greeks would build a sanctuary of Athena on a city's highest spot (like the Parthenon in Athens, on the Acropolis). Paestum had no hill, so the Greeks created a mound. The hill was more impressive in its time because the Greek city level was substantially lower than the Roman pavement stones you'll walk on today.

• *From here, walk about 100 yards down Via Sacra toward the other Greek temples. To the left of the road, you'll see a little half-buried house with a tiled roof.*

Greek Memorial Tomb: This tomb (from 500 B.C.) survived because the Romans respected religious buildings. But the tomb was most inconveniently located, right in the middle of their growing city. So the practical Romans built a perimeter wall around it (visible today), added a fine tiled roof, and then buried the tomb.

There's a mystery here. Greeks generally buried their dead outside the city (as did Romans)—there are over a thousand ancient tombs outside Paestum's walls—yet this tomb was parked smack-dab in the center of town. When it was uncovered in 1952, no bodies were found inside. The tomb instead held nine perfectly preserved vases (now in the museum). Archaeologists aren't sure of the tomb's purpose. Perhaps it was a memorial dedicated to some great hero (like a city founder). Or perhaps it was a memorial to those lost when a neighboring community had to evacuate and settle as refugees here.

• *Continue walking down Via Sacra, the main drag of...*

Roman Paestum: Roman towns were garrison towns: rectangular with a grid street plan and two main streets cutting north-south and east-west, dividing the town into four equal sections. They were built by military engineers with a no-nonsense standard design. New excavations (on the left) have uncovered Roman-era lead piping. City administration buildings were on the left, and residential buildings were on the right.

Shortly after the road turns into a dirt path, you'll come to a big Roman pool that archaeologists believe was a sanctuary dedicated to Fortuna Virilis, goddess of luck and fertility. The strange stones likely supported a wooden platform for priests and statues of gods. Imagine young women walking down the ramp at the far end and through the pool, hoping to conceive a child.

The next big square is the Roman Forum and ancient Paestum's main intersection. The road on the right led directly (and very practically) to the port. It made sense to have a direct connection to move freight between the sea and the center of town.

Until 2007, the vast field of ruins between the forum and the next temple (on the right) was covered in vegetation. It's recently been cleared, and cleaned of harmful lichen, which produce acids that dissolve limestone. Study the rocks: Yellow lichen is alive, black is dead. Even the great temples of Paestum were covered in this destructive lichen until 2000, when a two-year-long project cleaned them for the first time.

• *Ahead on the left are the so-called...*

Temples of Neptune and Hera: The **Temple of Neptune**

dates from 450 B.C. and employs the Greek architectural trick where the base line is curved up just a tad, to overcome the illusion of sagging caused by a straight base. The Athenians built their Parthenon (with a similar bowed-up base line) just 30 years after this. Many think this temple could have been their inspiration.

The adjacent **Temple of Hera,** dating from 550 B.C., is the oldest of Paestum's three temples and one of the oldest Greek temples still standing anywhere. Notice the change 100 years makes in the architectural styles: Archaic Doric in 550 B.C. versus Classic Doric in 450 B.C.

Archaeologists now believe the "Temple of Neptune" was actually devoted to a different god. Votive statues uncovered here suggest that Hera was the focus (perhaps this was a new and improved version of the adjacent, simpler, and older Temple of Hera). Or perhaps it was a temple to Zeus, Hera's husband, to honor the couple together.

Together, the two temples formed a single huge sanctuary with altars on the far (east) side. Walk around to the front. Notice how overbuilt the Temple of Hera appears. Its columns and capitals are closer together than necessary, as if the builders lacked confidence in their ability to span the distance between supports. Square pillars mark the corners of the *cella* inside. Temples with an odd number of columns (nine) had a single colonnade crossing in the center inside to support the wooden roof. More modern temples had six columns, with two colonnades passing through the *cella*. This left a line of vision open through the middle so that worshippers could see the big statue of the god.

By the way, in 1943, Allied paratroopers dropped in near here during the famous "Landing of Salerno." The Temple of Hera served as an Allied military tent hospital. From here the Allies pushed back the Nazis, marching to Naples, Cassino, and finally to Rome.

• *Leave the site and turn left on the modern road, Via Magna Grecia. The king of Naples built this Naples-to-Paestum road in 1829 to inspire his people with ancient temples. While he was modern in his appreciation of antiquity, his road project destroyed a swath of the ancient city. Just past the amphitheater, you'll find the...*

Ekklesiasterion: Immediately across the street from the museum is what looks like a sunken circular theater. This rare bit of ancient Greek ruins was the Ekklesiasterion, a meeting place where the Greeks would get together to discuss things and vote. Archaeologists believe that the Agora (market) would also have been located here.

• *Across the street is the...*

Paestum Archaeological Museum

Paestum's museum offers the rare opportunity to see artifacts—dating from prehistoric to Greek to Roman times—at the site where they were discovered. These beautifully crafted works (with good English descriptions throughout) help bring Paestum to life.

Before stepping into the museum, notice the proud fascist architecture. While the building dates from 1954, the design is pre-WWII fascist. It seems to command that you *will* enjoy this history lesson.

The exhibit is on several levels. You'll find mostly Greek pieces on the ground floor (artifacts from the Temple of Hera in front, frescoes from tombs in the back), Paleolithic to Iron Age artifacts on the mezzanine level, and Roman art on the top floor (statues, busts, and inscriptions dating from the time of the Roman occupation). While Roman art is not unique to Paestum, the Greek collection is—so that's what you should focus on. Here are the highlights:

Temple Reliefs: Wrapping around the first room, the large carvings overhead once adorned a sanctuary of the goddess Hera (wife of Zeus) five miles outside the city. Some of the carvings show scenes from the life of Hercules.

• *In the back of this room are glass cases holding nine perfectly preserved...*

Vases: One ceramic and eight bronze, with artistic handles, these vases were found in Paestum's Greek Memorial Tomb (described earlier). Greek bronzes are rare because Romans often melted them down to make armor. These were discovered in 1952, filled with still-liquid honey and sealed with beeswax. The honey (as you can see in the display cases below) has since crystallized. Honey was a standard part of a funeral because, to ancient Greeks, honey symbolized immortality...it lasts forever.

• *The next room is filled with ancient Greek...*

Votive Offerings: These were dug up around the Temple of Hera. Such offerings are a huge help to modern archaeologists, since the figures worshippers brought to a temple are clues as to which god the temple honored. These votives depict a woman with a crown on a throne—clearly Hera. The clay votives were simple, affordable, and accessible to regular people.

• *The next room holds...*

Temple Ornaments: The temples were once adorned with decorations, such as these ornamental spouts that spurted rainwater out of lions' mouths. Notice the bits of the surviving black, red, and white paint, and the reconstructions showing archaeologists' best guesses as to how the original decorations might have looked.

• *In a glass case nearby, find the statue of...*

Zeus: This painted clay statue of Zeus dates from 520 B.C. The king of the gods was so lusty with his antics, he's still smirking.

• *Look out the museum's back window for a good...*

View of Ancient Paestum: The walls of ancient Paestum reach halfway to the mountain—a reminder that most of the site is still private property and yet to be excavated. The town up on the mountainside is Capaccio, established in the eighth century when inhabitants of the original city of Paestum were driven out by malaria and the city was abandoned.

• *Along the corridor are...*

Objects from Tombs: Over 1,000 tombs have been identified outside of the ancient city's wall. About 100 were found decorated with frescoes or containing objects such as these.

• *At the end of the corridor is...*

The Tomb of the Diver: This is the museum's treasure and the most precious Paestum find. Dating from 480 B.C., it's not only the sole ancient Greek tomb fresco in the museum—it's the only one ever found in southern Italy. Discovered in 1968, it has five

frescoed slabs (four sides and a lid; the bottom wasn't decorated). The Greeks saw death as a passage: diving from mortality into immortality...into an unknown world. Archaeologists believe that the pillars shown on the fresco represent the Pillars of Hercules at Gibraltar, which in ancient times defined the known world. The ocean beyond the Mediterranean was the great unknown...like the afterlife. The Greek banquet makes it clear that this was an aristocratic man.

• *After the Tomb of the Diver, a room displays...*

Lucanian Tomb Frescoes: The many other painted slabs in the museum date from a later time, around 350 B.C., when Paestum fell under Lucanian rule. These frescoes are cruder than their earlier Greek counterpart. The people who conquered the Greeks tried to appropriate their art and style, but lacked the Greeks' distinctive light touch. Still, these offer fascinating glimpses into ancient life here at Paestum.

Sleeping in Paestum

(€1 = about $1.40, country code: 39)

Paestum at night, with views of the floodlit ruins, is magic.

$ Il Granaio dei Casabella, a converted old granary, is close to the action and reasonably priced. It has a beautiful garden, a nice restaurant, and views of one of the ancient temples from a corner of the property (Sb-€60-80, Db-€80-100, €120 in Aug, Wi-Fi, just west of the bus stop closest to Salerno at Via Tavernelle 84, tel. 082-872-1014, fax 082-881-1893, www.ilgranaiodeicasabella.com, info@ilgranaiodeicasabella.com, hospitable Celardo family).

$ Hotel Villa Rita is a tidy, quiet country hotel set on two acres within walking distance of the beach and the temples. It has 19 bright, modern, air-conditioned rooms; a kid-friendly swimming pool; and free parking (Sb-€70, Db-€90-100, €130 in Aug, third bed-€15, lunch or dinner-€16, Luigi promises a 10 percent discount with this book and cash in 2012, Wi-Fi, closed Nov-Feb, Via Nettuno 9, tel. 082-881-1081, fax-082-872-2555, www.hotel villarita.it, info@hotelvillarita.it). The hotel is a 10-minute walk west of the Hera entrance and public bus stop, and a 15-minute walk from the train station.

$ Hotel delle Rose, with 10 small, basic rooms with miniscule bathrooms, is near the Neptune entrance on the street bordering the ruins (Sb-€35, Db-€60, Luigi promises these prices in 2012 if you mention this book, Via Magna Grecia 193, tel. 082-8199-0692, www.hotelristorantedellerose.com/home.html, info@hotelristorantedellerose.com)

AMALFI COAST

Nearby

$$ Agriturismo Seliano offers plush public spaces, a pool, and 14 spacious rooms on a peaceful, ramshackle, once-elegant farm estate that's been in the same family for 300 years (Db-€80-100, €120 in Aug, air-con, serves a fine €20 lunch or dinner with produce fresh from the garden and all your drinks, closed Nov-March; one mile north of ruins on main road—Via Magna Grecia—a small *Azienda Agrituristica Seliano* sign directs you down long dirt driveway, best for drivers; tel. 082-872-3634, www.agriturismoseliano .it, seliano@agriturismoseliano.it). The place is run by Cecilia, an English-speaking baroness, and her family—including about a dozen dogs.

Paestum Connections

Salerno and Paestum

Salerno, the big city just north of Paestum, is the nearest transportation hub. From Naples or Sorrento, you'll change buses in Salerno to reach Paestum; from Naples or Pompeii, the train is easiest. Salerno's **TI** has bus, ferry, and train schedules (Mon-Sat 9:00-13:00 & 15:15-19:15, closed Sun, shorter hours off-season, on Piazza Veneto, just outside train station, tel. 089-231-432, toll-free 800-213-289, www.turismoinsalerno.it).

From Salerno to Paestum by Bus: Four companies (CSTP, SCAT, Giuliano, and Lettieri) offer a Salerno-Paestum bus service, all conveniently leaving from the same stop at Piazza della Concordia on the waterfront (2-3/hour, 50-70 minutes, schedules extremely sparse on Sun—better by train). Buy the €3 ticket on the bus, except for CSTP buses (buy these from the nearby tobacco shop). No clear schedule is posted at the Salerno stop. Simply ask a local or a bus representative at the stop for the next bus to Paestum; otherwise, get a schedule at the TI (more impartial, since they don't represent a particular company and their schedule shows all companies and times). Orange CSTP city buses use the same stop; ignore these.

When leaving Paestum, catch a northbound bus from either of the intersections that flank the ruins (see map on page 109). Flag down any bus, ask "Salerno?" and buy the ticket on board (except for CSTP buses—buy ticket at bar closest to stop).

From Salerno to Paestum by Train: The train from Salerno to Paestum (nearly hourly, 35 minutes, direction: Paola or Sapri) runs less frequently than the buses, though it's a quicker ride because it's immune to traffic jams; check schedules at Salerno's TI or train station. Paestum's ruins are an eight-minute walk from the train station (from station, go through old city wall, ruins are straight ahead). If you plan to leave Paestum by train, buy your

train ticket at the bar-café near the TI, because the station is not staffed (train schedules at TI). Leaving Paestum, trains bound for Salerno (direction: Battipaglia) usually continue to Naples.

From Naples to Salerno by Train: Trains run frequently (2/ hour, 45-75 minutes), but don't board the extra-slow *diretto* train. Note that some trains stop at Pompeii, and some continue to Paestum—ideal if you want to avoid a transfer.

From Sorrento to Salerno by Bus: The scenic three-hour Amalfi Coast drive (blue or green-and-white SITA bus, in peak season 20/day, 3 hours, easy transfer in Amalfi) drops you at Piazza della Concordia (where you can catch a bus to Paestum— see above). The stop is a few blocks from the Salerno train station, where the TI is located.

Buses from Salerno to Sorrento (and points in between) stop directly in front of Salerno's train station exit, on the median strip under the *Fermata SITA* sign. Buy your bus ticket at the newsstand inside the train station and tell the vendor your destination (prices vary). If it's closed, try the ticket windows in the train station or walk two blocks to Bar Cioffi (CHOH-fee), across the square from

Piazza della Concordia (see map on previous page). Ticket vendors change periodically; if Bar Cioffi no longer sells tickets, ask anyone, such as a clerk at a tobacco shop or magazine shop, "Who sells bus tickets to _?" by saying, *Chi vende i biglietti dell'autobus per ?* (kee VEHN-dee ee beel-YET-tee del-OW-toh-boos pehr).

From Sorrento to Salerno by Train: Ride the Circumvesuviana to Naples' Centrale station (2/hour, 70 minutes) and catch the Salerno train (2/hour, 45 minutes).

From Salerno by Ferry to: Amalfi (6/day, 35 minutes, €7), **Positano** (4-6/day, 70 minutes, €11), **Capri** (2/day, 2 hours, €16). Boats run mid-April through September with fewer boats off-season. Most ferries depart from Salerno's Piazza della Concordia, shown on the map on the previous page (tickets and info at TravelMar, Piazza della Concordia, tel. 089-872-950, www.travelmar.it). Boats to Capri depart from the part of Salerno's port called Molo Manfredi, about a mile west of Piazza Concordia, and are operated by Gescab (www.gescab.it).

Drivers: While the Amalfi Coast is a thrill to drive off-season, summer traffic is miserable. From Sorrento, Paestum is 60 miles and three hours via the coast, but a much smoother two hours by autostrada. To reach Paestum from Sorrento via the autostrada, drive toward Naples, catch the autostrada (direction: Salerno), skirt Salerno (direction: Reggio), exit at Battipaglia, and drive straight through the roundabout. During your ride, you'll see many signs for *mozzarella di bufala*, cheese made from the milk of water buffalo. Try it here—it can't be any fresher.

PRACTICALITIES

This section covers just the basics on traveling in Italy (for much more information, see *Rick Steves' Italy*). You can find free advice on specific topics at www.ricksteves.com/tips.

Money

Italy uses the euro currency: 1 euro (€) = about $1.40. To convert prices in euros to dollars, add about 40 percent: €20 = about $28, €50 = about $70. (Check www.oanda.com for the latest exchange rates.)

The standard way for travelers to get euros is to withdraw money from a cash machine (called a *bancomat* in Italy) using a debit or credit card, ideally with a Visa or MasterCard logo. Before departing, call your bank or credit-card company: Confirm that your card will work overseas, ask about international transaction fees, and alert them that you'll be making withdrawals in Europe.

Your US credit card might not work at some stores or at automated machines (e.g., train and subway ticket machines, luggage lockers, toll booths, parking garages, and self-serve gas pumps), because they're designed to accept European credit cards with a PIN code. If your card doesn't work, you have several options: Pay with euros, try your PIN code (ask your credit-card company in advance or use a debit card), or find a nearby cashier who should be able to process the transaction.

To keep your valuables safe, wear a money belt. But if you do lose your credit or debit card, report the loss immediately to the respective global customer-assistance centers. Call these 24-hour US numbers collect: Visa (410/581-9994), MasterCard (636/722-7111), and American Express (623/492-8427).

Phoning

Smart travelers use the telephone to reserve or reconfirm rooms, reserve restaurants, get directions, research transportation connections, confirm tour times, phone home, and lots more.

To call Italy from the US or Canada: Dial 011-39 and then the local number. (The 011 is our international access code, and 39 is Italy's country code.)

To call Italy from a European country: Dial 00-39 followed by the local number. (The 00 is Europe's international access code.)

To call within Italy: Just dial the local number.

To call from Italy to another country: Dial 00 followed by the country code (for example, 1 for the US or Canada), then the area code and number. If you're calling European countries whose phone numbers begin with 0, you'll usually have to omit that 0 when you dial.

Tips on Phoning: To make calls in Italy, you can buy two different types of phone cards—international or insertable—sold locally at newsstands. Cheap international phone cards, which work with a scratch-to-reveal PIN code at any phone, allow you to call home to the US for pennies a minute, and also work for domestic calls within Italy. Insertable phone cards, which must be inserted into public pay phones, are reasonable for calls within Italy (and work for international calls as well, but not as cheaply as the international phone cards). Calling from your hotel-room phone is usually expensive, unless you use an international phone card. A mobile phone—whether an American one that works in Italy, or a European one you buy when you arrive—is handy, but can be pricey. For more on phoning, see www.ricksteves.com/phoning.

Emergency Telephone Numbers in Italy: For English-speaking **police** help, dial 113. To summon an **ambulance,** call 118. For passport problems, call the **US Embassy** (in Rome, 24-hour line—tel. 06-46741) or **US Consulates** (Milan—tel. 02-290-351, Florence—tel. 055-266-951, Naples—tel. 081-583-8111); or the **Canadian Embassy** (in Rome, tel. 06-854-441) or **Canadian Consulates** (Naples—tel. 081-401-338, Padua—tel. 049-876-4833). For other concerns, get advice from your hotel.

Making Hotel Reservations

To ensure the best value, I recommend reserving rooms in advance, particularly during peak season. Email the hotelier with the following key pieces of information: number and type of rooms; number of nights; date of arrival; date of departure; and any special requests. (For a sample form, see www.ricksteves.com/reservation.) Use the European style for writing dates: day/month/year. For example, for a two-night stay in July, you could request:

"1 double room for 2 nights, arrive 16/07/12, depart 18/07/12." Hoteliers typically ask for your credit-card number as a deposit.

In general, hotel prices can soften if you do any of the following: offer to pay cash, stay at least three nights, mention this book, or travel off-season. You can also try asking for a cheaper room (for example, with a bathroom down the hall), or offer to skip breakfast.

Eating

Italy offers a wide array of eateries. A *ristorante* is a formal restaurant, while a *trattoria* or *osteria* is usually more traditional and simpler (but can still be pricey). Italian "bars" are not taverns, but small cafés selling sandwiches, coffee, and other drinks. An *enoteca* is a wine bar with snacks and light meals. Take-away food from pizza shops and delis (such as a *rosticcería* or *tavola calda*) makes an easy picnic.

Italians eat dinner a bit later than we do; better restaurants start serving around 19:00. A full meal consists of an appetizer (antipasto), a first course (*primo piatto*, pasta or soup), and a second course (*secondo piatto*, expensive meat and fish dishes). Vegetables *(verdure)* may come with the *secondo* or cost extra, as a side dish *(contorni)*. The euros can add up in a hurry, but you don't have to order each course. My approach is to mix antipasti and *primi piatti* family-style with my dinner partners (skipping *secondi*). Or, for unexciting but basic values, look for a *menù turistico* (or *menù del giorno*), a three- or four-course, fixed-price meal deal.

Good service is relaxed (slow to an American). You won't get the bill until you ask for it: *"Il conto?"* Most restaurants include a service charge in their prices (check the menu for *servizio incluso*—generally around 15 percent). If the menu states *servizio non incluso*, or *servizio* with a specific percentage, a fixed percentage (usually 10–15 percent of the total) will be added as a line item to the bottom of the bill. In either case, the total you pay already includes a basic tip. To reward good service, you can round up to the nearest euro.

At bars and cafés, getting a drink while standing at the bar *(banco)* is cheaper than drinking it at a table *(tavolo)* or sitting outside *(terrazza)*. This tiered pricing system is clearly posted on the wall. Sometimes you'll pay at a cash register, then take the receipt to another counter to claim your drink.

Transportation

By Train: In Italy, most travelers find it's cheapest simply to buy train tickets as they go. To see if a railpass could save you money, check www.ricksteves.com/rail. To research train schedules, visit Germany's excellent all-Europe website, http://bahn.hafas.de /bin/query.exe/en, or Italy's www.trenitalia.com (domestic journeys only).

You can buy tickets at train stations (at the ticket window or at automated machines with English instructions) or from travel agencies. Before boarding the train, you must validate your train documents by stamping them in the yellow box near the platform. Strikes *(sciopero)* are common and generally announced in advance (but a few sporadic trains still run—ask around).

By Car: It's cheaper to arrange most car rentals from the US. For tips on your insurance options, see www.ricksteves.com/cdw. Theft insurance is mandatory in Italy ($15–20/day). Bring your driver's license. You're also technically required to have an International Driving Permit—a translation of your driver's license (sold at your local AAA office for $15 plus the cost of two passport-type photos; see www.aaa.com). For route planning, try www.viamichelin.com. Italy's freeway *(autostrada)* system is slick and speedy, but you'll pay about a dollar for every 10 minutes of use. Be warned that car traffic is restricted in many city centers—don't drive or park in any area that has a sign reading *Zona Traffico Limitato* (*ZTL*, often shown above a red circle)...or you might be mailed a ticket later. A car is a worthless headache in cities—park it safely (get tips from your hotel). As break-ins are common, be sure all of your valuables are out of sight and locked in the trunk, or even better, with you or in your hotel room.

Helpful Hints

Theft Alert: Italy has particularly hardworking pickpockets. Assume beggars are pickpockets and any scuffle is simply a distraction by a team of thieves. If you stop for any commotion or show, put your hands in your pockets before someone else does. Better yet, wear a money belt.

Time: Italy uses the 24-hour clock. It's the same through 12:00 noon, then keep going: 13:00, 14:00, and so on. Italy, like most of continental Europe, is six/nine hours ahead of the East/West Coasts of the US.

Business Hours: Many businesses are open throughout the day Monday through Saturday, but some businesses close for lunch (roughly 13:00-15:30), particularly in smaller towns.

Sights: Opening and closing hours of sights can change unexpectedly; confirm the latest times with the local tourist information office or its website. Some major churches enforce a modest dress code (no bare shoulders or shorts) for everyone, even children.

Holidays and Festivals: Italy celebrates many holidays, which can close sights and attract crowds (book hotel rooms ahead). For information on holidays and festivals, check Italy's website: www.italiantourism.com. For a simple list showing major—though not all—events, see www.ricksteves.com/festivals.

Numbers and Stumblers: What Americans call the second

floor of a building is the first floor in Europe. Europeans write dates as day/month/year, so Christmas is 25/12/12. Commas are decimal points and vice versa—a dollar and a half is 1,50, a thousand is 1.000, and there are 5.280 feet in a mile. Italy uses the metric system: A kilogram is 2.2 pounds; a liter is about a quart; and a kilometer is six-tenths of a mile.

Resources from Rick Steves

This Snapshot guide is excerpted from the latest edition of *Rick Steves' Italy,* which is one of more than 30 titles in my series of guidebooks on European travel. I also produce a public television series, *Rick Steves' Europe,* and a public radio show, *Travel with Rick Steves.* My website, www.ricksteves.com, offers free travel information, a Graffiti Wall for travelers' comments, guidebook updates, my travel blog, an online travel store, and information on European railpasses and our tours of Europe. If you're bringing a mobile device on your trip, you can download free information from Rick Steves Audio Europe, featuring podcasts of my radio shows, free audio tours of major sights in Europe, and travel interviews and other audio content about Italy (via www.ricksteves.com/audioeurope, iTunes, or the Rick Steves Audio Europe free smartphone app).

Additional Resources

Tourist Information: www.italiantourism.com
Passports and Red Tape: www.travel.state.gov
Packing List: www.ricksteves.com/packlist
Cheap Flights: www.skyscanner.net
Airplane Carry-on Restrictions: www.tsa.gov/travelers
Updates for This Book: www.ricksteves.com/update

How Was Your Trip?

If you'd like to share your tips, concerns, and discoveries after using this book, please fill out the survey at www.ricksteves.com/feedback. Thanks in advance—it helps a lot.

PRACTICALITIES

Italian Survival Phrases

Good day.	**Buon giorno.**	bwohn JOR-noh
Do you speak English?	**Parla inglese?**	PAR-lah een-GLAY-zay
Yes. / No.	**Si. / No.**	see / noh
I (don't) understand.	**(Non) capisco.**	(nohn) kah-PEES-koh
Please.	**Per favore.**	pehr fah-VOH-ray
Thank you.	**Grazie.**	GRAHT-seeay
You're welcome.	**Prego.**	PRAY-go
I'm sorry.	**Mi dispiace.**	mee dee-speeAH-chay
Excuse me.	**Mi scusi.**	mee SKOO-zee
(No) problem.	**(Non) c'è un problema.**	(nohn) cheh oon proh-BLAY-mah
Good.	**Va bene.**	vah BEHN-ay
Goodbye.	**Arrivederci.**	ah-ree-vay-DEHR-chee
one / two	**uno / due**	OO-noh / DOO-ay
three / four	**tre / quattro**	tray / KWAH-troh
five / six	**cinque / sei**	CHEENG-kway / SEHee
seven / eight	**sette / otto**	SEHT-tay / OT-toh
nine / ten	**nove / dieci**	NOV-ay / deeAY-chee
How much is it?	**Quanto costa?**	KWAHN-toh KOS-tah
Write it?	**Me lo scrive?**	may loh SKREE-vay
Is it free?	**È gratis?**	eh GRAH-tees
Is it included?	**È incluso?**	eh een-KLOO-zoh
Where can I buy / find...?	**Dove posso comprare / trovare...?**	DOH-vay POS-soh kohm-PRAH-ray / troh-VAH-ray
I'd like / We'd like...	**Vorrei / Vorremmo...**	vor-REHee / vor-RAY-moh
...a room.	**...una camera.**	OO-nah KAH-meh-rah
...a ticket to ___.	**...un biglietto per ___.**	oon beel-YEHT-toh pehr
Is it possible?	**È possibile?**	eh poh-SEE-bee-lay
Where is...?	**Dov'è...?**	DOH-veh
...the train station	**...la stazione**	lah staht-seeOH-nay
...the bus station	**...la stazione degli autobus**	lah staht-seeOH-nay DAYL-yee OW-toh-boos
...tourist information	**...informazioni per turisti**	een-for-maht-seeOH-nee pehr too-REE-stee
...the toilet	**...la toilette**	lah twah-LEHT-tay
men	**uomini, signori**	WOH-mee-nee, seen-YOH-ree
women	**donne, signore**	DON-nay, seen-YOH-ray
left / right	**sinistra / destra**	see-NEE-strah / DEHS-trah
straight	**sempre diritto**	SEHM-pray dee-REE-toh
When do you open / close?	**A che ora aprite / chiudete?**	ah kay OH-rah ah-PREE-tay / keeoo-DAY-tay
At what time?	**A che ora?**	ah kay OH-rah
Just a moment.	**Un momento.**	oon moh-MAYN-toh
now / soon / later	**adesso / presto / tardi**	ah-DEHS-soh / PREHS-toh / TAR-dee
today / tomorrow	**oggi / domani**	OH-jee / doh-MAH-nee

In an Italian Restaurant

I'd like...	**Vorrei...**	vor-REHee
We'd like...	**Vorremmo...**	vor-RAY-moh
...to reserve...	**...prenotare...**	pray-noh-TAH-ray
...a table for one / two.	**...un tavolo per uno / due.**	oon TAH-voh-loh pehr OO-noh / DOO-ay
Non-smoking.	**Non fumare.**	nohn foo-MAH-ray
Is this seat free?	**È libero questo posto?**	eh LEE-bay-roh KWEHS-toh POH-stoh
The menu (in English), please.	**Il menù (in inglese), per favore.**	eel may-NOO (een een-GLAY-zay) pehr fah-VOH-ray
service (not) included	**servizio (non) incluso**	sehr-VEET-seeoh (nohn) een-KLOO-zoh
cover charge	**pane e coperto**	PAH-nay ay koh-PEHR-toh
to go	**da portar via**	dah POR-tar VEE-ah
with / without	**con / senza**	kohn / SEHN-sah
and / or	**e / o**	ay / oh
menu (of the day)	**menù (del giorno)**	may-NOO (dayl JOR-noh)
specialty of the house	**specialità della casa**	spay-chah-lee-TAH DEHL-lah KAH-zah
first course (pasta, soup)	**primo piatto**	PREE-moh peeAH-toh
main course (meat, fish)	**secondo piatto**	say-KOHN-doh peeAH-toh
side dishes	**contorni**	kohn-TOR-nee
bread	**pane**	PAH-nay
cheese	**formaggio**	for-MAH-joh
sandwich	**panino**	pah-NEE-noh
soup	**minestra, zuppa**	mee-NEHS-trah, TSOO-pah
salad	**insalata**	een-sah-LAH-tah
meat	**carne**	KAR-nay
chicken	**pollo**	POH-loh
fish	**pesce**	PEH-shay
seafood	**frutti di mare**	FROO-tee dee MAH-ray
fruit / vegetables	**frutta / legumi**	FROO-tah / lay-GOO-mee
dessert	**dolci**	DOHL-chee
tap water	**acqua del rubinetto**	AH-kwah dayl roo-bee-NAY-toh
mineral water	**acqua minerale**	AH-kwah mee-nay-RAH-lay
milk	**latte**	LAH-tay
(orange) juice	**succo (d'arancia)**	SOO-koh (dah-RAHN-chah)
coffee / tea	**caffè / tè**	kah-FEH / teh
wine	**vino**	VEE-noh
red / white	**rosso / bianco**	ROH-soh / beeAHN-koh
glass / bottle	**bicchiere / bottiglia**	bee-keeAY-ray / boh-TEEL-yah
beer	**birra**	BEE-rah
Cheers!	**Cin cin!**	cheen cheen
More. / Another.	**Ancora un po.' / Un altro.**	ahn-KOH-rah oon poh / oon AHL-troh
The same.	**Lo stesso.**	loh STEHS-soh
The bill, please.	**Il conto, per favore.**	eel KOHN-toh pehr fah-VOH-ray
tip	**mancia**	MAHN-chah
Delicious!	**Delizioso!**	day-leet-seeOH-zoh

For more user-friendly Italian phrases, check out *Rick Steves' Italian Phrase Book & Dictionary* or *Rick Steves' French, Italian, and German Phrase Book.*

INDEX

INDEX

Rick's free app and podcasts

The FREE **Rick Steves Audio Europe**™ app for iPhone, iPad and iPod Touch gives you 29 self-guided audio tours of Europe's top museums, sights and historic walks—plus more than 200 tracks filled with cultural insights and sightseeing tips from Rick's radio interviews—all organized into geographic-specific playlists.

Let **Rick Steves Audio Europe**™ amplify your guidebook.

With Rick whispering in your ea Europe gets even better.

Thanks Facebook fans for submitting photos while on location! From top: John Kuijper in Florence, Brenda Mamer with her mother in Rome, Angel Capobianco in London, and Alyssa Passey with her friend in Paris.

Find out more at ricksteves.com

Join a Rick Steves tour

Enjoy Europe's warmest welcome... with the flexibility and friendship of a small group getting to know Rick's favorite places and people. It all starts with our free tour catalog and DVD.

Great guides, small groups, no grumps.

Free information and great gear

▸ Plan Your Trip

Browse thousands of articles and a wealth of money-saving tips for planning your dream trip. You'll find up-to-date information on Europe's best destinations, packing smart, getting around, finding rooms, staying healthy, avoiding scams and more.

▸ Eurail Passes

Find out, step-by-step, if a railpa makes sense for your trip—and how to avoid buying more than y need. Get free shipping on online orders

▸ Graffiti Wall & Travelers Helpline

Learn, ask, share—our online community of savvy travelers is a great resource for first-time travelers to Europe, as well as seasoned pros.

NOW AVAILABLE:
eBOOKS, APPS & BLU-RAY

eBOOKS

Most guides are available as eBooks from Amazon, Barnes & Noble, Borders, Apple, and Sony. Free apps for eBook reading are available in the Apple App Store and Android Market, and eBook readers such as Kindle, Nook, and Kobo all have free apps that work on smartphones.

RICK STEVES' EUROPE DVDs

10 New Shows 2011–2012
Austria & the Alps
Eastern Europe
England & Wales
European Christmas
European Travel Skills & Specials
France
Germany, BeNeLux & More
Greece & Turkey
Iran
Ireland & Scotland
Italy's Cities
Italy's Countryside
Scandinavia
Spain
Travel Extras

BLU-RAY

Celtic Charms
Eastern Europe Favorites
European Christmas
Italy Through the Back Door
Mediterranean Mosaic
Surprising Cities of Europe

PHRASE BOOKS & DICTIONARIES

French
French, Italian & German
German
Italian
Portuguese
Spanish

JOURNALS

Rick Steves' Pocket Travel Journal
Rick Steves' Travel Journal

APPS

Select Rick Steves guides are available as apps in the Apple App Store.

PLANNING MAPS

Britain, Ireland & London
Europe
France & Paris
Germany, Austria & Switzerland
Ireland
Italy
Spain & Portugal

Rick Steves books and DVDs are available at bookstores and through online booksellers.

Avalon Travel
a member of the Perseus Books Group
1700 Fourth Street
Berkeley, CA 94710

Printed in the United States by Worzalla

ISBN 978-1-59880-683-0

For the latest on Rick's lectures, guidebooks, tours, public radio show, and public television
series, contact Europe Through the Back Door, Box 2009, Edmonds, WA 98020, tel.
425/771-8303, fax 425/771-0833, www.ricksteves.com, rick@ricksteves.com.

Europe Through the Back Door Reviewing Editors: Risa Laib, Jennifer Madison Davis,
Cameron Hewitt
ETBD Editors: Gretchen Strauch, Cathy McDonald, Suzanne Kotz, Cathy Lu, Tom
Griffin
Research Assistance: Ian Watson, Ben Cameron, Karin Kibby, Helen Inman, Kat Reno,
Claire Burns
Avalon Travel Senior Editor and Series Manager: Madhu Prasher
Avalon Travel Project Editor: Kelly Lydick
Copy Editor: Patrick Collins
Proofreader: Nöel Chrisman
Indexer: Stephen Callahan
Production and Typesetting: McGuire Barber Design
Cover Design: Kimberly Glyder Design
Graphic Content Director: Laura VanDeventer
Maps & Graphics: David C. Hoerlein, Laura VanDeventer, Twozdai Hulse, Lauren Mills,
Barb Geisler, Kat Bennett, Mike Morgenfeld, Brice Ticen
Photography: Rick Steves, Gene Openshaw, David C. Hoerlein, Laura VanDeventer,
Cameron Hewitt, Jennifer Hauseman, Dominic Bonuccelli, Michael Potter, Les
Wahlstrom, Robyn Cronin, Ben Cameron, Ian Watson, Bruce VanDeventer, Anne
Jenkins, Wikimedia Commons
Cover Photo: A view along the Amalfi Coast, Italy © Alison Brice/Dreamstime.com
Title Page Photo: Piazza del Plebiscito, Naples, Italy © edella/www.123rf.com